ROUTLEDGE LIBRARY EDITIONS:
KUWAIT

I0130491

Volume 3

KUWAIT CITY PARKS

KUWAIT CITY PARKS

A critical review of their design,
facilities, programs
and management

SUBHI ABDULLAH AL-MUTAWA

Routledge
Taylor & Francis Group

LONDON AND NEW YORK

First published in 1985 by KPI Limited

This edition first published in 2018
by Routledge
2 Park Square, Milton Park, Abingdon, Oxon OX14 4RN

and by Routledge
711 Third Avenue, New York, NY 10017

Routledge is an imprint of the Taylor & Francis Group, an informa business

British Library Cataloguing in Publication Data
A catalogue record for this book is available from the British Library

ISBN: 978-1-138-62956-1 (Set)
ISBN: 978-1-315-15946-1 (Set) (ebk)
ISBN: 978-1-138-06520-8 (Volume 3) (hbk)
ISBN: 978-1-138-06533-8 (Volume 3) (pbk)
ISBN: 978-1-315-15980-5 (Volume 3) (ebk)

Publisher's Note
The publisher has gone to great lengths to ensure the quality of this reprint but points out that some imperfections in the original copies may be apparent.

Disclaimer
The publisher has made every effort to trace copyright holders and would welcome correspondence from those they have been unable to trace.

Kuwait City Parks

A critical review of their design,
facilities, programs
and management

Subhi Abdullah Al-Mutawa

KPI

*London, Boston, Melbourne
and Henley*

*Published in association with
Kuwait University*

First published in 1985 by KPI Limited
14 Leicester Square, London
WC2H 7PH, England

Distributed by
Routledge & Kegan Paul plc
14 Leicester Square, London
WC2H 7PH, England

Routledge & Kegan Paul
9 Park Street Boston, Mass. 02108, USA

Routledge & Kegan Paul
464 St Kilda Road, Melbourne,
Victoria 3004, Australia and

Routledge & Kegan Paul plc.
Broadway House, Newtown Road,
Henley on Thames, Oxon RG9 1EN, England

Produced by Worts-Power Associates
Printed in Great Britain
by Redwood Burn Ltd

ISBN 07103-0068-9

Acknowledgements

I dedicate this research to Linda, my wife, and to my two children Tariq and Shannon.

Also, I would like to give special thanks to Dr Robert Aukerman, Dr Arthur Wilcox, Dr Howard Aldenand Dr Dick Walsh. Special thanks, also, to Mr Saleh Shehab, Assistant Under-Secretary for Recreation and Tourism for the State of Kuwait.

Contents

List of Tables

Table

List of Figures

Part 1

Introduction

Objective

The objective of this study was to investigate the current management practices of the Kuwait park system and the relationship of these practices to user satisfaction. The investigation included all of the agencies involved with the quality of park design, facilities, programs, and management. Recommendations are provided to the involved agencies which could improve the decision making process and result in higher user satisfaction.

In order to understand this study, the reader must first become aware of the geographical location, topography, climate, government, economy and culture of Kuwait. These factors are important as they have a profound influence on the type and extent of recreation opportunities in Kuwait.

Geographical Orientation

Kuwait is situated at the northeastern section of the Arabian Peninsula, between latitudes 28°35' to the south and 30°05' to the north, and between longitudes 46°30' to the west and 48°30' to the east of Greenwich (Central Statistical Office, 1978). It is bounded on the east by the Arabian Gulf, on the southwest by the Kingdom of

Saudi Arabia, and on the north and west by the Republic of Iraq. Its territory occupies about 17,000 square kilometers.

Several islands are scattered in the Arabian Gulf. At the entrance of the Bay of Kuwait is the densely populated Failaka Island. Inside the Bay of Kuwait are two smaller islands, Korein and Om-Al-Namel which are located near the Shuwaikh Coast (Figure 1).

The coast of Kuwait is mostly sand beach which is part of the Arabian desert, but there are some coral reefs, of an appreciable size, scattered along the southern shore. Several sandy lagoons are found along the coast, among them, an inlet at Khor Al-Khiran beach, which may be of some significance to recreation. The Bay of Kuwait, 40 kilometers long and 25 kilometers wide at the mouth, is surrounded by sand beach and marsh (Katsuzo et al., 1972).

There are no rivers or streams in Kuwait, but scattered fresh water wells exist in the desert.

Topography

Kuwait is generally flat, broken only by occasional low hills and shallow depressions. Elevations range from sea level in the east to nearly 300 meters in the southwestern part of the country. Generally, the land surface slopes northeastward.

The Jal Az-Zor Slope forms one of the few prominent topographic features of the country. Another feature is the Ahmadi Ridge which rises gently to a height of 137 meters, separating the oil fields of Burgan from the coast. There is only one large depression, called Wadi Al-Batin, which borders the western section of the country. Wadi Al-Musannat, which crosses the southern border near Manageesh, is less clearly defined.

In the central section of Kuwait there are no distinct features, but in the coastal areas, large patches of salt marsh have developed under the influence of marine groundwater (Werner et al., 1968) (Figure 2).

Climate

Kuwait's climate is a desert type, characterized by extremely hot dry summers with the average daily temperatures of 45°C. and mild to cool winters with an average temperature of 3°C. The annual rainfall

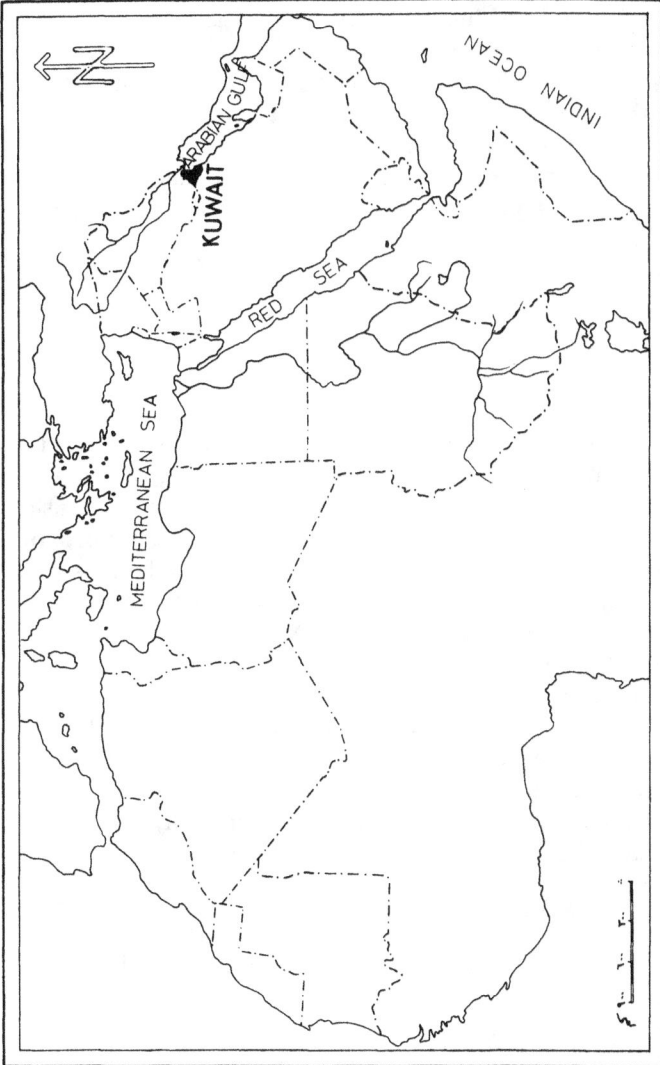

Figure 1: *Kuwait geographical location*

varies from 8 cm to 33 cm and occurs during the winter and spring months, November and April (Werner et al., 1968). During the summer, Kuwait experiences two kinds of weather. The first begins during the months of June and July, with dry and hot northwesterly winds (simoom) prevailing with dust storms common (Central Statistical Office, 1978). The second period, called the humid period, begins the 20th of July and continues until the end of October. The hot season generally extends to the end of October when the temperature is ranging between 20–30°C. The nights are generally cool with warm days. This period, between the 5th of November and the 5th of December, is called autumn.

Government

According to the Constitution of 1962, the executive power in the state of Kuwait is vested in the Amier (the head of the state), who exercises his authority through a Council of Ministers. The legislative power is exercised by the National Assembly, composed of 50 members elected every four years. The Assembly passes bills, approves the budget, and may withdraw confidence and force any minister to resign. The country is divided into 10 regions, each represented by 5 members in the Assembly.

The Amier has the authority to return any bill to the National Assembly for reconsideration before ratification, but the bill would automatically become law if it is passed by two-thirds majority (Arab Information Center, 1972).

The management of the park system is especially affected by the governmental organization and will be discussed in more detail later (see Figure 3).

Economy

The economy has depended heavily on the oil industry as Kuwait is third among the Middle Eastern countries in oil production. It is ranked seventh in world oil production and fifth among oil exporting countries (Central Statistical Office, 1978). Because of oil revenue, the people of Kuwait enjoy the second highest per capita income in

4

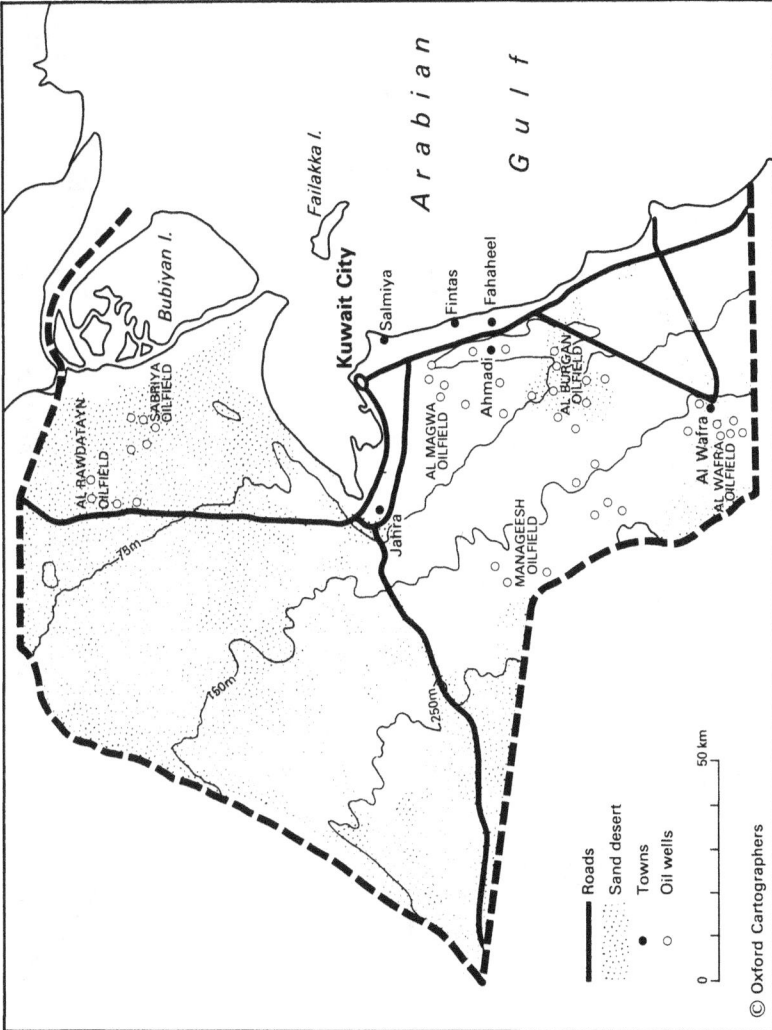

Figure 2: *Topographical map of the state of Kuwait*

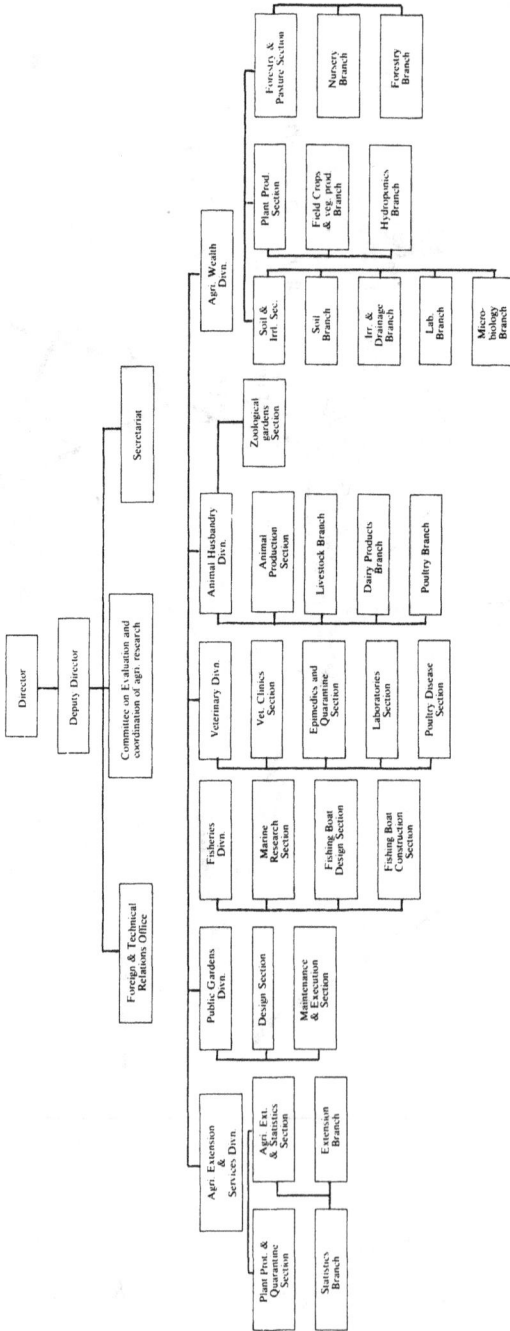

Figure 3: *Ministry of Public Works, Department of Agriculture organizational chart.*

the world, and are provided with many social services either free or at a minimum cost. Health service and education are free.

The government of Kuwait is trying to reduce the country's dependence on oil by encouraging and participating in the establishment of both oil-related and non-oil-related industries. The scarcity of raw materials other than oil and natural gas, and the high labor costs impose limitations to industrial growth.

Agriculture represents a very small part of the Kuwaiti economy. This is caused by deficiencies of soil, scarcity of irrigation water, climatic conditions and the limited supply of manpower trained in agricultural skills. However, cultivatible areas and agricultural production have recently realized some expansion. Local production of vegetables now represents about 46% of the total domestic consumption, fish 99%, poultry 34%, milk 41% and eggs 18% (Central Statistical Office, 1978).

A healthy Kuwait economy has freed many people to use the recreational facilities and opportunities in Kuwait. This has put pressure on management agencies to provide more and better recreational programs.

Culture

Kuwait is made up of many nationalities and cultures. However, it was not always this way. Until 1899 Kuwait was inhabited by tribes of pure Arab descent, who lived mainly off the sea as fishermen, pearl divers, or ship builders. Their lifestyle was one of simplicity and deep religious faith. These early inhabitants were "Sunie", a sect of the Moslem religion. Families and the community were closely knit, and everyone knew everyone else.

In 1899 the British became a protector for Kuwait. At that point Kuwait began to be a country inhabited with "ajaneb" or foreigners. Several British at the time made Kuwait their home, and some of their European lifestyles started showing up in Kuwait homes. A few English words began to invade the Arabic language.

Kuwait was, however, to receive its largest influx of foreigners in 1936 when large quantities of oil were found. From that time, people from all over the world came to the country. In 1979 there were 480,000 Kuwaitis and 520,000 non-Kuwaitis, the latter comprising 52% of the population. This foreign population was comprised of

Population by Sex and Nationality

السكان حسب النوع والجنسية

Census 1965, 1970, 1975

Nationality	Percent 1975 Census	Percent 1970 Census	Percent 1965 Census	Census 1975 Total	Census 1975 Female	Census 1975 Male	Census 1970 Total	Census 1970 Female	Census 1970 Male	Census 1965 Total	Census 1965 Female	Census 1965 Male	الجنسية
Arab Nationalities													
Kuwaitis	47.5	47.0	47.1	472,088	235,488	236,600	347,396	171,883	175,513	220,059	107,490	112,569	كويتيون
Jordan & Palestine	20.5	20.0	16.6	204,178	96,408	107,770	147,696	67,762	79,934	77,712	27,968	49,744	الأردن وفلسطين
Iraq	4.5	5.3	5.5	45,070	18,571	26,499	39,066	15,483	23,583	25,897	10,135	15,762	العراق
Saudi Arabia	1.3	1.5	1.0	12,527	5,907	6,620	10,897	4,872	6,025	4,632	1,751	2,881	السعودية
Lebanon	2.5	3.4	4.5	24,776	11,568	13,208	25,387	11,242	14,145	20,877	8,057	12,820	لبنان
Syria	4.1	3.7	3.6	40,962	16,321	24,641	27,217	10,037	17,180	16,849	4,774	12,075	سوريا
Egypt	6.1	4.1	2.4	60,534	24,739	35,795	30,421	13,029	17,392	11,021	5,225	5,796	جمهورية مصر العربية
Tunis	*	*	–	127	54	73	74	24	50	–	–	–	تونس
Algeria	*	*	*	69	27	42	113	23	90	75	3	72	الجزائر
Libya	*	*	–	46	26	20	10	4	6	–	–	–	ليبيا
Morocco	*	*	–:	59	21	38	40	8	32	–	–	–	المغرب
Sudan	0.2	0.1	0.1	1,553	434	1,119	773	211	562	418	79	339	السودان
P.D.R. Yemen	1.2	1.2	0.6	12,332	2,021	10,311	8,604	765	7,839	2,635	75	2,560	اليمن الجنوبية
Arab Yemen R.	0.5	0.3	*	4,831	1,076	3,755	2,363	337	2,026	144	11	133	الجمهورية العربية اليمنية
Bahrain	0.1	0.1	0.2	1,359	790	569	966	457	509	747	306	441	البحرين
Qatar	*	*	*	112	50	62	117	38	79	159	61	98	قطر
Arab Gulf Emirates	0.3	0.6	0.2	2,585	1,203	1,382	4,435	1,590	2,845	1,105	283	822	الإمارات العربية
Muscat & Oman	0.7	2.0	4.2	7,313	2,196	5,117	14,670	2,238	12,432	19,584	2,736	16,848	مسقط وعُمان
Other Arabs	0.1	–	1.3	754	350	404	–	–	–	6,068	95	5,973	حسابات عربية أخرى
Non Kuwaiti Arabs	42.1	42.4	40.2	419,187	181,762	237,425	312,849	128,120	184,729	187,923	61,559	126,364	غير الكويتيين العرب
Total Arab Nationality	89.6	89.4	87.3	891,275	417,250	474,025	660,245	300,003	360,242	407,982	169,049	238,933	جملة الجنسيات العربية

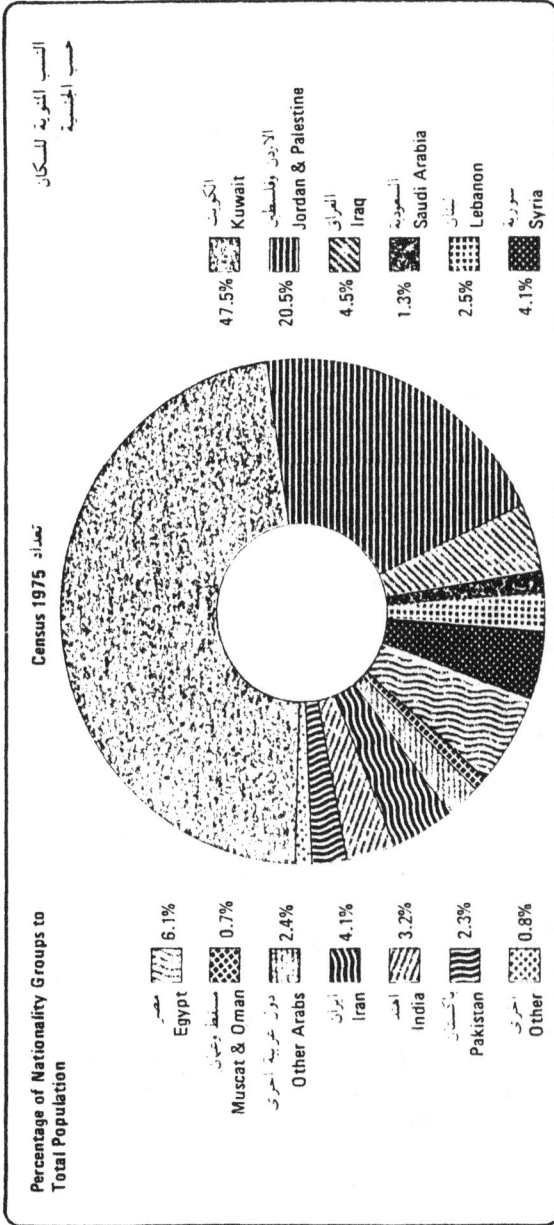

Figure 4: *Percentage of nationality groups to total population by sex*

Europeans, Americans, Orientals, Indians, Pakistanis and other Arab nationalities (see Figure 4). These different peoples brought with them a wide diversity of cultures.

As a result of these influences, Kuwait has a mixture of old Arab culture existing side by side with modern European culture. An example of this is high rise shopping centers with stores carrying the latest fashion from Paris and London situated next door to the "Old Market" where vendors sit in stalls selling fresh fruits and vegetables.

Another influence on Kuwaitis is from their children. Most Kuwaiti young receive their higher education abroad. They bring back many foreign ideas from the country where they studied. Also, many of the Kuwaiti males marry foreign girls and bring them home.

Not only has the traditional Kuwaiti culture been altered, but also the bloodlines have been broken. We now have in Kuwait, many mixed marriages whose children grow up with a bi-cultural background. These children have a tendency to extend this bi-culture to older relatives such as grandparents and uncles.

The nation is faced with the problems caused by the mixing of the old and the new. The question is how to plan and be able to satisfy both old and young, traditional and non-traditional, and deeply religious and non-religious. In earlier times, Kuwaitis did not socialize with the foreign groups, although they assimilated some of their culture. However, now the children bring foreign culture into their homes. In the old culture, women had their own social gatherings, while the men had their separate groups. Family life was very close. The older Kuwaitis want to see this continued; however, the children feel otherwise.

Young women are now given equal opportunity for education as well as work. Most are not willing to be told by their parents that they must obey the old culture. They want to associate with both their female and male peers. They do not want to be separated by sex as they feel they are now equal. They work side by side with male counterparts all day, and are unwilling to be separated when it comes to a social function.

The older generation sees this as a breakdown in morals due to outside influences. The younger generation sees it as inevitable modernization for the overall benefit of the country.

Planners and administrators dealing with the public must decide how to plan for the 48% Kuwaitis or the 52% foreigners knowing that part of the 48% Kuwaitis lean toward foreign attitudes. This is a difficult situation.

10

Recreation

The recreational movement began with the beginning of the country in 1756, and has its roots deep in the remote past and is a product of a variety of conditions and social forces. Changes in attitude toward recreation have been traced historically.

The geography and topography of Kuwait placed a limit on the recreational activities which could occur. Most activities were oriented toward the sea, including fishing, boating, swimming, and picnicking. Fishing, swimming and boating were predominantly male-oriented activities for cultural and religious reasons. Those water-oriented activities took place during the summer season when ideal weather permitted. Yet, during the winter and spring, the desert is a haven for other types of activities with the whole family participating. Horseback riding, hunting, sport-oriented games and picnicking were all popular.

People moved to the desert during the winter and spring to escape the cold and humid weather associated with the coast. The further one moves away from the sea during the winter and spring, the milder the weather can be; just the opposite of the summer. Wildlife also migrate from the neighboring countries into Kuwait where the weather is more favorable. This provides the people with further opportunities for recreational hunting.

Until 1930, the population of the country was about 250,000 people. At that time, life was simple due to the lack of technology and modernization. People viewed recreation as playing games and considered it a normal family activity. Since the discovery of oil in the mid-1930s, many people from outside the country have been attracted to Kuwait. People came to seek employment or were brought in by the government as experts in developing the country and its resources. Foreigners brought different cultures, customs, and most of all, different recreational activities such as water skiing, scuba diving, sailing, deep sea fishing, parachute jumping, bicycling, car racing, and others.

The introduction of new technology, like electricity, television and theaters, introduced still other types of recreation. The increased availability of money to the Kuwaitis also gave them the opportunity to travel and to see other countries. This exposure to other cultures through travel and the presence of foreigners introduced a wide mixture of ideas. For example, the influence of other cultures and technology can be witnessed by changes in the architecture of

Kuwaiti homes. Old Arabic and Spanish architecture has given way to other modern European styles. The foreign culture has also affected recreation. Leisure activities changed from simply desert and coastal-oriented activities to European style sea clubs which provide recreation for each member of the family. These activities ranged from swimming, fishing, boating, and water skiing to bowling.

The educational system also contributed to changes in recreational activities. Since over 80% of the school teachers were foreigners, part of their culture was introduced into the schools. This can be seen by the introduction of playground facilities to the schools. The success and the acceptance of the playgrounds spread all over the country, encouraging people in the recreational field to duplicate such facilities and use them in public parks.

Recently, opportunities for recreation have become much greater than before due to the increased incomes, leisure time and exposure to other cultures. Government as well as private agencies were forced by public demand for recreation to adopt new recreational programs or contribute assistance to existing ones.

Study Scope

The study was applied to three Kuwait City urban parks, the Greenbelt, the Sheraton, and the Municipality Park. The study was concerned with park visitor satisfaction with parks' design, facilities, programs and management. The study analyzed the positive and negative aspects of the most preferred parks in reference to these factors. However, the study was not concerned about the least preferred parks due to both the limited time and funds available for the research during the summer of 1979.

Part 2

Review of Literature on Decision Making and Survey Techniques

The literature review for this study has four objectives:
1. the decision making process and conflict;
2. survey techniques;
3. USA community surveys, and;
4. the Kuwait park survey.

The first objective was met by reviewing the literature and decision making processes and the procedures that should be followed for obtaining good decisions. The related literature on conflict and its resolution was examined to obtain suggestions for making good decisions where conflicts exist. Also, the reason for looking at the decision making process and conflict was to determine if good decisions had been made for Kuwait's parks in the past.

The second objective was met by reviewing literature on survey techniques in order to determine the appropriate techniques that could be used in Kuwait.

The third objective was met by reviewing the recreation surveys conducted by the Glencoe Park and Recreation District and LaSalle District in Illinois. The author believed that some of their techniques might be used as guidelines for designing the Kuwait research project.

The fourth objective was met by reviewing the 1974 Kuwait urban parks research, to determine its validity and relevance to the present study.

Decision Making Process and Conflict

A review of the literature on decision making was considered relevant to this study of the situation in Kuwait. The quality of the decision making process in Kuwait directly affected the parks. Also, it provided a basis for looking at conflicts between individuals and the organization that might be as a result of incompatible resources, problems of status and differences of perception. A study of the decision making process in Kuwait also offers a perception of whether good coordination and communication exists during conflict, and offers ideas on how to improve the coordination and communication between the conflicting parties.

Decision Making

Minute management decisions that govern specific actions are inevitably instances of the application of broader decisions relative to the purpose of planning and management (Simon, 1976). An important element of decision making is the element of compromise (i.e., the process of choosing among various alternatives). The final selection of the alternative never permits a complete or a perfect achievement of all the objectives, but it can be considered as the best solution that is available under a specific circumstance.

The environmental situation, the number of agencies involved, and the relationship between the various objectives can greatly complicate the decision making process. Under these complications, managers must make plans and implement decisions. The process of choosing between alternatives can be broken down into sequential steps. However, the theories for choosing alternatives can vary from the three-step models of John Dewey (1933) and Herbert Simon (1978) to more complex, five-step models developed by systems theorist Alva Elbing (1970).

John Dewey (1933) developed a three-stage process for decision making. First, a controversy must exist as opposite ideas regarding the same objective. Secondly, there must be a clarification and process for defining these alternatives. Thirdly, a choice between the ideas must be made to solve the disputed parties and solve as a rule or principal for future decisions.

However, Simon (1976) considered as the most widely known

decision theorist, indicated that there should be three stages in the decision making process. His stages are:

1. Intelligent activities. The manager should search the work environment for ways that could improve the conditions of that environment which may require new decisions.
2. Design activities. This could be approached by developing, inventing, or analyzing various alternatives that lead to the improvement of that environment.
3. Choice activities. This type of activity is considered to be the most important stage in decision making. It is approached by selecting the appropriate course of action to be followed from all available analyzed alternatives that lead to the improvement of the environment.

A comprehensive approach developed by Elbing (1970) was the use of system analysis. The five-step system which Elbing feels the management decision maker is affected by is:

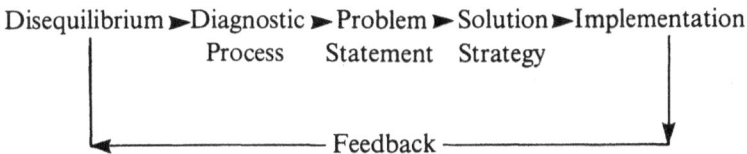

Disequilibrium ➤ Diagnostic ➤ Problem ➤ Solution ➤ Implementation
Process Statement Strategy
⎯⎯⎯⎯⎯⎯⎯ Feedback ⎯⎯⎯⎯⎯⎯⎯

Elbing, in his model, indicated that the manager sometimes experiences feelings of disequilibrium and regards some situations as problem situations. The response to the disequilibrium in this case is to diagnose the problem which caused the disequilibrium. Then, define the problem that needs to be solved. The manager then selects a method and a solution to solve the disequilibrium. Finally, implementation of the decision is made, whether or not it actually leads to the solution of the problem that caused disequilibrium. However, in looking at decision making as a process, the choice will be a continuous feedback of information for implementing the decision.

Thus, decision making is a dynamic process. Whether expressed in simple steps used by Dewey and Simon, or in more complex steps as described by Elbing, there are some identifiable introductory steps that lead to the selection of alternatives in decision making. However, these steps become more realistic when presented in a time sequence:

1. The past – where the problems originated and the need to have a decision made.

2. The present – when alternatives have to be identified and the best alternative is selected.
3. The future – when the decision is implemented. The important point is that decision making processes are composed of a series of related steps. Each step depends upon the previous one.

Gortner (1977) defined disequilibrium as the state of non-balance or non-adjustment between two conflicting opinions or parties. Disequilibrium, as a condition, can come to an administrator's attention from either inside or outside of the organization. Wherever a conflict in opinion originates, the administrator should immediately clarify the situation to eliminate the existing conflict or disequilibrium. Once an understanding of the existing conflict has been developed, the decision makers can determine what steps are appropriate to resolve the conflict. By examining and selecting among different alternatives, a decision can be made which will most likely resolve the conflict, and hopefully re-establish equilibrium.

This procedure can be followed in making any decision, whether by a single administrator or many agencies.

Dalton McFarland (1970) proposed that basic decisions require long term commitments or a major investment of the agency's resources in such a way that some mistakes might only temporarily affect the main objective of the agency. Jubenville (1978) indicated that in outdoor recreation there are four types of decisions which vary in degree of importance. These decisions include:

1. Primary decisions. These determine the main, long range objectives of the agency. These are formed by the integration of many programs that direct the agencies toward their main objectives.
2. Problem oriented decisions. Such decisions can be obtained by analyzing and correcting each and every specific problem in order to achieve the long range objectives of the agency.
3. Task oriented decisions. These decisions are made by lower level management and are routine in nature. However, the primary and problem oriented decisions are obtained by the high level management.
4. Reflex decisions. These are considered the lowest level of decision making in the outdoor recreation system due to their simplicity and routine nature.

Jubenville (1978) outlined the decision making process and the type of decisions that can be made in outdoor recreation. It is possible that the same techniques can be applied in most any organization even though the objectives might be different. However, Gortner (1977) believes that:

> "Many decisions are doomed to failure at the instant they are made because the decision maker has based the final choice on the attitudes and values he holds, and takes it for granted that the other individuals involved agree with those ideas. Attitudes and values are often projected from one individual to another; however, attitudes are deeply personal and differ to some extent for each individual (p. 117)."

This attitude may be projected to: 1) other administrators within an agency; 2) other administrators in other agencies, or; 3) the public. In any case, this projection of attitude may cause a faulty decision. This can be related to: 1) inefficient communication among the higher levels of management; 2) the unity of command concept where authority is misused and communication is ignored from the lower level of management, or; 3) the irrational decisions made by higher levels of management which prevent implementation of decisions by lower levels of management.

The disequilibrium or conflict suggested by Gortner (1977) which can exist in an organization can be further discussed to obtain better understanding about how and why conflicts exist, and how they can be solved. In Kuwait, the decision making process for the parks is fragmented among three agencies: the Department of Agriculture, Ministry of Municipality, and Ministry of Information. Each agency has a different function, therefore they have different goals for the parks. As a result, the quality of the decision making for the parks has become very poor. By investigating the decision making process, and taking into account how good decisions are reached, as suggested by Elbing, Simon, Dewey and Jubenville, and through their decision making model, a better decision can be reached for Kuwait City parks.

Conflict

Conflict is a vital aspect of organizational behavior. In order to understand conflict it must be realized that every person has a number of competing needs and roles, and he can express these drives and roles in various ways. A person sometimes comes upon barriers

17

that block him from obtaining his goals.

Luthans (1977) indicated that there can be several aspects of conflict, such as the intra-individual, interpersonal or organizational perspectives.

In intra-individual conflict, we may find frustration, goal conflict or role conflict. Frustration is caused when efforts are blocked before obtaining the goal. Goal conflict can be brought on by approach-approach, approach-avoidance, or avoidance-avoidance situations. Berelson and Steiner (1964) explained that approach-approach conflict is when a person has two or more positive goals to choose from. This conflict is not hard to solve and usually the individual will convince himself that one goal is more appropriate than the other goal. They also stated that the approach-avoidance conflict is when a person is trying to obtain a goal, but feels that the time is not appropriate to do so. This type of conflict is most relevant to the analysis of organizational behavior.

In avoidance-avoidance conflict, Luthans (1977) showed that this kind of conflict occurs when there are two negative goals. A person may not choose either of them and may simply leave the situation. This type of conflict is usually easily solved. However, this is not usually the type that can exist in an organization.

Another factor of intra-individual conflict is role conflict. Everyone plays various roles in their life which may conflict with each other. Filley and House (1969) said that when the conflicted roles arise the extent of undesirable effects depends on four major variables: 1) the awareness of role conflict; 2) acceptance of conflicting job pressure; 3) ability to tolerate stress; and 4) general personality make-up.

The second aspect of conflict is the interpersonal conflict which arises from the interaction of two or more persons. Kelly (1974) noted that:

> "Conflict situations inevitably are made up of at least two individuals who hold apparently polarized points of view, who are somewhat intolerant of ambiguities, who ignore delicate shades of gray, and who were quick to jump to conclusions (p. 563)."

Interpersonal conflict can be put into three categories according to the outcome. These are the lose-lose, win-lose, and win-win situations. In the lose-lose situation the middle ground may be taken, bribery may be used, or a third party brought in to arbitrate. This is sometimes the only way the conflict can be ended, but this is the least desirable resolution as one idea overpowers the other. This is common and can often be seen in union management relations. Such lose-lose resolution of conflict can be beneficial as well as negative. It creates competitions which may lead to progressive outcomes. However, someone must lose and this can bring jealousy and bitter feelings.

After review of relevant literature, Filley, House and Kerr (1976) concluded that the most desirable outcome is the win-win situation from a human and organizational standpoint. In this situation the parties involved worked together to a rewarding end for those involved.

Conflict in organizations is similar to conflict between individuals. This point was stressed by Boulding (1963) when he says:

"Much of the theory of conflicting organizations... applies equally well either to organizations or to persons. The main differences lie in the greater capacity of organizations for growth and, therefore, for incompatibility in their self-images. Persons are sharply limited in extent by their biological structure; organizations are much less limited in this way, though, even here the biological limits on the capacity for the receipt of information and for the elaboration of images may be important. For this reason, organizational conflict is likely to be more extensive, more diffuse, and perhaps more dangerous than the conflict of persons. It is not, however, an essentially different system (p. 165)."

There are two types of conflict that can occur in an organization. One is conflict between organizations and the other is conflict within the organization itself. Conflict among organizations is common and goes hand in hand with free enterprise and competition. Competition could be for: 1) scarce resources; 2) drives for autonomy, or the attempt to gain control over organizational programs, and; 3) differences of opinions among various groups. The reaction to conflict from the organization is the same as from the individuals, but with greater intensity. Therefore, organizations are characteristically faced with more conflict than can be dealt with in a given time. Litterer (1969) suggested four causes of organizational conflict: 1) an incompatible goal situation; 2) the existence of incompatible means of incompatible resource allocation; 3) a problem of status incongruities, and; 4) a difference of perceptions. These sources of conflict in the organization result from the dynamics of individuals and group interactions. However, conflict can originate in the organization in four structural areas; 1) hierarchial conflict, where conflict may exist between the various levels of the organization; 2) functional conflict, where conflict may exist between the various functional departments of the organization; 3) line-staff conflict, where conflict may exist between line and staff. In some cases staff personnel may not have the authority or the control over line personnel; and 4) formal-informal conflict, where conflict may exist between the formal and informal organizations due to their incompatible norms for performance.

The methods of handling conflict are changing. Previously, conflict was thought to be avoidable and strict adherence to the rules was emphasized and trouble makers were eliminated. Emphasis was on a chain of hierarchy. Authority and structure were used to solve problems.

Today, behaviorists are looking at conflict from an almost opposite point of view (Luthans, 1977). They believe conflict should be expected and that it has some benefit to the organization. Forward movement through conflict is an integral process of success.

Litterer (1965) suggested three basic strategies to reduce organizational conflict: 1) erect buffers between the conflicting parties; 2) help the parties in the conflicting situation develop better insights into themselves and how they affect others, and; 3) redesign the organizational structure to reduce the conflict.

When considering conflict and its impact on an organization, it should be noted that it may have either desirable or undesirable effects. Management can be the balancer and, depending on its decision making, may improve the organization or detract from it.

If conflict is not handled correctly, it can lead to a decrease in productivity and quality of programs. Conflict can lead to divisions of individuals within the organization, and a breakdown in communication (Pondy, 1967).

However, if handled right, conflict will be positive. According to Kelly (1969): 1) conflict is inevitable; 2) the causes of conflict can be found only by examining the total situation; 3) conflict is one of the primary elements in bringing about needed changes, and, therefore: 4) conflict may be good for the organization and may be a sign of proper management.

Conflict is vital to the organization's growth as long as it results in working for the goals desired and not creating a hinderance to the achievement of these goals. If conflict is handled properly and channeled into the right direction it can be beneficial. Gortner (1977) stated that:

> "The way the conflict is resolved and the effect of the
> conflict on the well being of the bureaucracy are directly
> traceable to the way the organization is equipped to cope
> with the problem. In turn, the organization's ability to cope
> with conflict is controlled by the personality and skills of the
> top manager (p. 209)."

Most organizations have channels through which the conflict is handled. The individuals within the organization have roles, rules and norms that they follow. If the organization does not have a well established set of channels, it can be destroyed by inner turmoil and pressure for power. The top administrators carry the main responsibility of dealing with the resolution of conflict in the organization. He is the negotiator for internal affairs, and for dealing with other organizations.

The administrator must communicate what the organization stands for, what its goals are and how best to achieve them. He must also be willing to accept suggestions from others on how best to attain these goals.

Conflict is present among the three agencies involved in the decision making process for Kuwait parks. Since each agency has a different function and goal, their attitudes toward the parks are also in conflict with each other. The Department of Agriculture's attitude is that the parks are to beautify the cities first and second for public use. However, the Ministry of Municipality and the Ministry of Information share a similar attitude toward the parks; that the parks are for public use first and second to beautify the cities. This conflict in attitudes creates a lack of communication between them. The literature shows how conflict can exist and how it can be resolved. The procedure in conflict resolution can be followed to reduce the existing conflict in order to enhance the decision making process for Kuwait parks.

Survey Techniques

Community surveys play an important part in providing data dealing with all aspects of recreation. Most of the surveys conducted in the United States dealing with recreation have been done by direct observation, mailed questionnaires, telephone surveys and personal interviews. The literature review for this study indicated that many recreational interests can be found in any population (Miller, 1973). Various survey techniques will be discussed in detail and the reason explained why each was or was not applied in Kuwait.

Observational Technique

The observational technique can be applied to assess the type and extent of recreational activities in which people most often participate. This method is useful when literature or documents concerning recreation activities are not in existence (such as in Kuwait) or when accurate information cannot be obtained by other methods. For example, there are several reasons why the observational technique can be considered superior to the interview. Often when collecting information by interview, the respondent can be so involved in an activity that he or she is not willing to be interviewed. Secondly, cultural background, habits or physical behavior might form a barrier between the respondent and the interviewer. In these situations the use of the observational technique is preferable, especially if the respondent is unwilling or unable to respond to questioning.

However, the observational technique does have limitations. In addition to the limitations placed on this method by the amount of time involved, this manner of surveying cannot be used to study feelings, beliefs, values, attitudes or cognitive processes. Another problem with this method is related to the observer's cultural background. If the observer comes from a culture that is different from that of the participant, information which seems clear to the observer might have a totally different meaning to the participant. And, although the observational technique can be applied to assess the recreational activities in which people most often participate, it cannot indicate participants' reactions to recreational activities, design, facilities, programs or regulations (Moser and Kalton, 1971).

22

The observational method cannot be used exclusively in Kuwait City because of the difficulty in getting Kuwaiti people to collect information in this manner. Therefore, most of the people hired to do the surveying will be non-Kuwaitis. This makes the observational method unreliable and nonpreferable since most non-Kuwaitis are either not familiar with all cultures or they are biased towards their own culture. This restriction would apply to Kuwaitis as well since 52% of the population is non-Kuwaiti.

Mail Questionnaires

Mail questionnaires are popular in the educational and recreational fields. But, because of some of the difficulties in obtaining adequate response rates, this method of gathering data may be inappropriate in Kuwait. Although some high response rates have been achieved in recent mail surveys (Moser and Kalton, 1971) to significantly reduce this argument, the difficulty of obtaining good response rates remains a serious problem. The literature indicated that mail questionnaires were considered to be generally cheaper and less time consuming, which makes this method of obtaining information attractive to recreation researchers. All the questionnaires can be sent out at one time and often the responses can be received within a few weeks. The respondent may reply in his own time and give an accurate response. Mail questionnaires can also eliminate interviewer bias. Finally, the mail questionnaire will give greater assurance of anonymity because of the absence of the interviewer.

But the mail questionnaire also has disadvantages. First, the questionnaires are standardized and lack flexibility. If the respondent misunderstands the question, he or she will possibly misinterpret it or ignore it altogether. Secondly, a response rate of about 30 to 40% is considered to be adequate without follow-ups, while a response rate of about 70 to 80% has been achieved with follow-ups. Without these follow-ups a researcher sometimes has to contact a high number of people to obtain his desired number of responses.

In Kuwait the response rate is even lower. According to the planning board (1974) a return rate of only 10 to 15% can be expected in the best of circumstances, where the questionnaires are ideal and deal with a specific problem and not recreation in general.

Another drawback to using a mailed questionnaire in Kuwait is the country's cultural diversity and customs of its people. Kuwaiti culture places the male person in a superior position as the head spokesman for the household. Therefore, the mail questionnaires will most likely be answered by male members of the household and thereby biased in nature. This increases the problem caused by the diversity in cultures and how each culture perceives its recreation based on religious beliefs. To some families, recreation should not be part of their daily lives because it replaces religion with play. Therefore the mailed questionnaire will not be used in this study.

Telephone Survey

Telephone surveys can combine aspects of both mail questionnaires and personal interviews as Selltiz, Wrightsman and Cook (1976) noted:

> "Some social scientists have prejudices against the use of telephone interviewing that are not supported by evidence, or they hold beliefs that may have been true in the past but are no longer accurate. The major reservation about telephone interviewing has been that those people that have telephones are not representative of the population. This problem is still present to some degree, particularly in rural areas and in the inner city. A second problem is that an increasing proportion of telephone subscribers are maintaining unlisted numbers (p. 298)."

The advantage of the telephone interview is that it is inexpensive and is a fast way to obtain information. The telephone survey can gather sensitive information which the personal interview cannot because the respondent can remain anonymous and therefore will not consider the interview as a threat.

A disadvantage of the telephone interview is that the respondent might be distrustful, thinking that a prank is being played on him. Another limitation is the inability to show the respondent items such as checklists, diagrams or pictures which might help the respondent to give a more meaningful answer to some questions. Finally, the interviewer cannot have any control over the length of the interview since the respondent could hang up at any time.

In Kuwait, the telephone survey is inappropriate due to the fast development of the country and the resulting telephone network being far from perfect. The inadequacy of the telephone system was caused by the fast construction of new roads, highways and residential areas. This increase in construction put a limitation on the number of telephone lines that could be provided to the public. Almost all Kuwaitis have telephones in their homes but most non-Kuwaitis do not. This is because of the limited number of telephone lines and the high deposit required for non-Kuwaitis. Since most of the residents of Kuwait City are non-Kuwaiti and represent the major labor force in the country, a survey technique which left them out would not be representative.

The Personal Interview

Gorden (1969) noted that personal interview is considered the most important and valuable method for gathering information from the public. The oldest method known to social researchers for obtaining specific information, is superior to the telephone survey and the mailed questionnaire (Moser and Kalton, 1971). The personal interview is most flexible in that the interviewer can interact with the respondent and probe the respondents for answers to specific questions. This becomes very important to the researcher who deals with all types of people.

Gorden (1975) discussed interviewing, its relationship to other survey techniques, and its superiority over the other techniques. There are two types of interviews, first the standardized interviews which are designed to collect precise information from the respondents. Their answers can or should be compared and classified. In this technique, the differences in the answers are not due to the questionnaires but are due to the individual differences in the respondents (Selltiz, Wrightsman and Cook, 1976).

The other type of interview is the non-standardized. This method does not give or ask the same question to all the respondents, but each group or individual has different sets of questions which they answer. This method is not considered scientific because the dissimilarity in the content of the questions makes analyzing the information quantitatively and qualitatively difficult. However, some researchers consider this method valid because, in some cases, the non-standardized interview is conducted to prepare for the standardized questions. This technique was used by the author to explore and pinpoint the correct terminology to be used in the final sample.

Comparing the interview and the questionnaire, we find that information obtained from questionnaires is limited to the written responses. Because of the questionnaire's impersonal nature, standardized terminology and standardized instructions for recording responses are required. The researcher hopes to obtain uniformity in the answers to his questions.

From a psychological aspect, the uniformity may be real. However, because its standardized vocabulary may give diverse meanings to different individuals, uniformity depends on many variables such as culture, education and many others. Hopefully, by being able to explain questions that might otherwise be misunderstood, this problem can be avoided in the interview.

Another problem of the questionnaire and of the interview is establishing the feeling of confidentiality. Some of the interview respondents might consider the information which they reveal harmful to someone and therefore not answer some questions accurately. If the questionnaire respondents remain anonymous, the result can be of great importance. Hopefully, the interviewer can assure the respondent of the confidential nature of his answers.

Edward's (1975) techniques of attitude scale construction, for example, tried to measure people's attitudes to proposed state legislation. He attempted to survey the residents of Seattle by administering the questionnaire in two ways. One group of residents were questioned by the interviewer and the second group was given a sheet marked "secret ballot", on which the respondents checked answers and then deposited the questionnaires into a secret ballot box. His findings showed that answers which were obtained by the interviewer were more precise.   In Kuwait personal interviews can be considered an appropriate procedure that can be used for assessing people's recreational needs. As indicated, most of the non-Kuwaitis do not have telephones, or a permanent address in the city that an interviewer can reach them or select them properly. Then, it is logical that the personal interview can be an appropriate procedure.

Glencoe Park and Recreation District

A community survey was conducted in 1967 in Glencoe, Illinois, by the Field Service Department of Recreation and Park Administration, University of Illinois. The objective of the study was to answer

26

questions concerning public parks and recreational facilities, programs and services provided to the residents of the Glencoe Park and Recreation District. These questions were:

1. What was the range of leisure opportunities available in Glencoe?
2. What recreation activities did Glencoe adults and young say they participated in?
3. What did Glencoe adults and youth recommend for additional park facilities and recreation programs in the Glencoe Park District?
4. How sufficient did Glencoe adults and youth believe the Glencoe Park and Recreation District was in providing park facilities and recreation programs?

The research also had three auxiliary purposes which were:

1. to increase public involvement in the planning and decision making process;
2. to provide the professional staff and the community residents of Glencoe with a better understanding of public parks and recreation, and;
3. to provide supporting data to the governmental units of the Glencoe District.

To meet the study objectives, a survey questionnaire was designed by the faculty and graduate students of the Department of Recreation and Park Administration at the University of Illinois. The first part of the questionnaire was oriented toward the demographic variables in order to obtain information about community characteristic for both the adults and the youth. This information was helpful in basic planning procedures. It was also important to understand the sample when making generalizations about the total population.

The second part of the questionnaire was concerned with the time used during the day in any activities whatsoever. In order to plan programs or change the time when facilities should be available, it is necessary to know what the basic time-use patterns of the residents of any community are. The third part of the questionnaire considered leisure behavior. The information was based on frequency counts of the respondent in selected activities over a certain period of time. The adult respondents were also asked whether they belonged to any private clubs, whereas the youth respondents were asked what they did after school each day. This information was important to the planning agency which could provide them with some ideas of what people did during their leisure time.

A fourth section was concerned with leisure behavior attitudes as the agency was interested in the attitude of the respondents toward the district providing services within the community in general.

The last part of the questionnaire dealt with the community, facilities, and the recreational programs, and the community attitude toward the total Glencoe Park Recreation District system. Those questions were designed to elicit value judgement from each respondent.

The above information was important to the Glencoe District in that it provided an overall evaluation of the Park-Recreation District.

The sampling techniques used by Glencoe contained a random and systematic sampling technique. Using the formula developed by Yamane (1967) for confidence limits of 95% and specified reliability limits of ±5%, a sample size of 400 adults was needed, 564 youths from Glencoe fifth and sixth grades, 250 from seventh and eighth grades, and 500 from all the high schools in the village of Glencoe.

The adult sample was chosen by selecting every fifth person from a list of all individuals living within the Glencoe Park and Recreation District.

The questionnaires were distributed by 60 women volunteers from PTAs, Sacred Heart School, PTOs, the League of Women Voters and the garden clubs. The questionnaires were sent back by mail. The youth questionnaires, however, were administered by the school's principal in the area.

The village of Glencoe was divided into three communities. Originally, an attempt was made to collect data from each community. However, early analysis indicated there were no significant differences between the three communities. Therefore, the total population was analyzed instead of each community.

After recovering the questionnaires, the data was analyzed using sample frequency distribution, percentage and the means. Then, recommendations were made to Glencoe Park and Recreation District. However, the recommendations did not appear in their published reports (University of Illinois, Department of Recreation and Park Administration, 1967).

The Glencoe research can be considered a major contributing factor to the Kuwait study especially in the method of choosing their sample size, the survey techniques, and the design of their questionnaire. The Kuwait sample was selected according to the same formula table that is described in the methodology section. The survey technique used in Kuwait was the personal interview. The

Kuwait questionnaires were designed by the author and the graduate committee in the Department of Recreation Resources. However, Kuwait study did not use a mail survey due to the reason stated earlier. However, some questions in the Glencoe research were irrelevant to the Kuwait study. Different types of recreational activities, facilities used and the programs that are not applicable to Kuwait due to differences in Kuwait's topography and culture.

The Glencoe community survey indicated that when the population is heterogeneous, a stratified sampling technique can be used for studying the community. This can be done by dividing the community into separate neighborhoods, then studying each community separately.

Since Kuwait's population is heterogeneous, a stratified sampling technique was used to obtain maximum representation of the city population similar to Glencoe. The city was stratified into four segments consisting of the Greenbelt Park, Municipality Park, Sheraton Park, and government and private businesses. Early analysis of the Kuwait study indicated less than 15% of the sample did not visit any park. Therefore, only the park users are discussed. Analysis for each park was conducted.

LaSalle Community Survey

A community survey was conducted in LaSalle County Conservation District, Ottawa, Illinois, in 1968 by the University of Illinois, Department of Recreation and Park Administration. The objective of the study was to identify recreational goals and objectives of the district and to suggest a policy framework for future decisions. The study also indicated that recommendations for developing specific programs, facilities and administration mechanisms, as well as means for implementation would result. The intent for the study was to survey leisure behavior and attitudes, and to determine the needs and the desires of people in LaSalle County.

To this end, a set of questionnaires were designed by the University of Illinois researchers to include: 1) the availability of leisure time; 2) leisure behavior patterns; 3) facilities in the county; and 4) demographic variables. Although it is difficult to assess leisure behavior, the survey included questions on how people spent their vacations and weekends, the availability of time for recreation, the

29

type of recreational facilities owned, membership in a recreational club, activities they participated in, and what facilities they used. By asking specifically related questions, leisure behavior could be assessed.

The researchers decided that one large random sample should be taken from the population. But, due to the large sample and the high cost of interviewing, mail questionnaires were delivered. In order to reduce cost further, a group of community volunteers were assigned to deliver the questionnaires. A pretest of the questionnaires was conducted on 40 citizens from different ethnic backgrounds. Changes were made to improve the quality and the understanding of the question contents. Over 2,400 questionnaires were delivered and the return rate was less than 50%. In addition, some questionnaires took more than four months to be returned.

LaSalle County was divided into five separate strata or communities. Each strata was divided into urban community, rural-non-farm community, and rural community. However, no explanation was submitted on how the division in each strata was obtained.

The data was analyzed using sample frequency distribution and measures of central tendency. Cross-tabulation tables were also used to show the relationship between two or more related variables.

The result was presented in a formula that related each variable used in the study to the responsible demographic variables, and how the result could be related to the total population. The results showed that the people of LaSalle County could be considered somewhat different in their preferences for recreational activities, based on a comparison of LaSalle's top five outdoor leisure pursuits, with the U.S.A.'s trends. That comparison is shown below:

LaSalle County Top Five	*U.S.A. Top Five*
Driving for pleasure	Walking for pleasure
Fishing	Swimming
Picnicking	Driving for pleasure
Swimming	Outdoor games and sports
Walking	Bicycling

Three of the top five recreational activities were similar. This may be an indication of the limited availability of alternative facilities to the people. Yet, bicycling was considered of little importance to LaSalle people but was considered the fifth most popular in the nation according to the Bureau of Outdoor Recreation (1968).

The LaSalle study contributed to the present study in the designing of the questionnaires and pretesting them on small pilot groups. The pretesting is a good indication of the validity of the questionnaire. Although the LaSalle study could support the present study, they are different in their objectives, variables and the questionnaires. The distinction results from the different problems, culture, and recreational opportunities studied.

As indicated before, the Kuwait questionnaires were designed by the author, based on his cultural background, and his knowledge about Kuwait, and by the graduate committee at the Department of Recreation Resources (Colorado State University). This is an indication that the questions were valid and reliable. However, the Kuwait study used a similar pretest as LaSalle used. The pretest was used to find out whether the questionnaire was valid enough to be used in Kuwait, and also whether the wording was appropriate. Therefore, the LaSalle study can contribute to the validity of the Kuwait study.

Kuwait Urban Park Survey

Kuwait Planning Board Research

During the summer of 1974, the Ministry of Information, Department of Recreation and Tourism, with cooperation of the planning board in Kuwait, conducted research in Kuwait's urban parks dealing with park users. The project's major emphasis was on programming special activities selected and financed by the Department of Recreation and Tourism for public enjoyment. A survey questionnaire was designed by the statistician on the planning board to meet the objectives of the research. The objectives of the study were:

1. To determine the range of people's acceptance to different recreational programs and their attitude toward present recreational programs.
2. To measure leisure behavior, and to determine the needs of people in Kuwait for recreational programs.
3. To use the result of the study for future government recreational planning.

A sample of 2,000 persons was taken. Information was collected by 21 persons through personal interview in 15 urban parks. A pretest for the questionnaires was not conducted. The sample was randomly selected from people who were actually present in the park during special recreational programs. Two kinds of questions were used, open-ended and closed-ended.

The first part of the questionnaire dealt with the demographic variables. Questions were asked to determine whether the sample was representative of the whole population. That information was also used to determine the average age and level of education for assessing and planning the type and quality of future recreational programs.

The second part was concerned with leisure time and the activities which the respondent participated in during his/her leisure time. Included in this part were questions dealing with the present recreational programs, their quality and how to improve them. Given the format of the interview and the design of the questionnaire, there is some question about the reliability and validity of the data. Response bias may be present because all the questions required a positive response from the interviewee.

The third part was concerned with the parks in relation to management and facilities. There was only one question relating to the management in general, one question with maintenance and one with facilities.

The last part of the questionnaire contained the open-ended questions. Two questions were addressed to the respondents. The first one was concerned about the respondent's suggestion for improving recreational programs in general, and the second with any problems that faced the recreational programs.

The data were analyzed using frequency count and frequency distribution. The mean for each activity the respondent engaged in during the leisure time was given.

The research only reported their findings. No recommendation or discussion of their results were presented.

From a research standpoint, the 1974 planning board research concerning Kuwait parks can be considered a positive step toward recreational planning in Kuwait. Up to that period, there were no surveys dealing with urban park users or research done concerning any aspect of recreation. However, the research can be considered incomplete. The incompleteness of the study arose from the fact that the survey dealt with only one variable, programs, and did not consider the other recreation variables present in Kuwait. Thus, it can be considered a contribution to the present research. Since it was the first research in Kuwait, it is considered the foundation for the present one and is an indication that the officials in the government of Kuwait were interested in providing recreational opportunities for the people. But, due to lack of the professionals in the field of recreation, the study was not completed. However, the author felt that there was a need for conducting research dealing with the Kuwait City parks. This is why the planning board research can be considered as a starting point in studying and developing the recreational movement in Kuwait, and as a foundation for this study. None of the planning board data is used in this study due to the bias nature in collecting their data.

The final report dealing with recreational policy of April, 1975 (Planning Board, 1975) indicated that the 1974 planning board study was not completed and that the reason such research had not been approached before may be due to several factors:

1. lack of experts in the field of recreation;
2. lack of research dealing with recreation;
3. lack of trained personnel to conduct the survey (it was the first of its kind in Kuwait);
4. the survey was conducted during the first year of public programming. Since the programs were new and without change, the public may have felt that it was not kind to criticize the agencies involved or the programs, and that criticism might have caused cancellation of the free recreation programs. This may have resulted in biased answers to the questions.

The author believes the present research is timely. A lack of previous research and qualified manpower to conduct the research, coupled with increasing leisure time, and park visits, make this research important. This study goes beyond the 1974 research, thus, it can explore all the major variables involved directly or indirectly in recreation. By researching and evaluating past research and present methods dealing with recreation, a framework or planning method can be established for recreation in order to provide better parks and quality recreation experiences.

Summary

The literature indicated that an important element of decision making is the element of compromise. By identifying the problem, choosing between various alternatives and having continuous feedback, a good decision could be reached. However, this is not the case that existed in Kuwait parks. Each agency was determined to

33

implement their decision for providing recreational opportunities for the public. The element of compromise was not introduced in their decision and as a result, conflict was created due to different goals and attitudes. The literature, also, shows that conflict should be resolved by changing. If change is not introduced, the quality of the decision can be affected.

The literature also discussed all the survey techniques in providing data dealing with all aspects of recreation in order to determine the appropriate techniques that could be used in Kuwait. However, the personal interview was selected for the Kuwait study in order to obtain better and more reliable information about park users.

The literature also discussed the USA and Kuwait community recreational survey in order to have a better understanding of the way such surveys are conducted.

In conclusion, the literature review in this part will help the author to identify and understand the problems that exist in Kuwait, and by doing so provide better parks and a better quality of recreational experience.

Part 3

Methodology

The Problem

The government of Kuwait has no central agency dealing with recreation as its main function as several government agencies have joined together to provide recreational opportunities. This effort, even with its positive attitude towards recreational planning, has created many problems. For example, a diversity in opinion developed which may have created a lack of coordination among the agencies. Each agency usually insisted on using its own recreational plan so that it would receive credit for the work. Credit for the creation of a recreational plan meant more money and public support for that agency. That kind of competition created conflict and, in turn, hampered communication between the agencies. That lack of communication further contributed to the perpetuation of lack of coordination between the agencies.

It is possible that such a lack of communication and coordination could create public dissatisfaction with the parks in general. Therefore, there was a need to investigate the current system with all the agencies involved with the park design, facilities, programs and management. Based on the investigation, recommendations are provided to the involved agencies which could improve the decision making processes and result in higher user satisfaction.

Need for the Study

Given the problem of conflict between agencies which has created little coordination and less communication, the following are reasons why this study was needed:

1. The literature pointing out or documenting the problems are limited. The author's personal experience as a park user and as a government employee for the Department of Agriculture has pointed to the need for investigating the current system. The purpose of that investigation was to provide sound recreational opportunities for the public.

2. The absence of professional park planners or a central agency to look into the parks problem and user dissatisfaction was a contributing factor to the need for this study. The purpose was to investigate the source of problems and then to provide recommendations.

3. The unorganized decision making process for providing recreational opportunities suggested a need for improvement. The purpose of the investigation was to provide information to improve that process.

Objectives

The objectives of this study and the related hypotheses are:

1. To determine the degree of user satisfaction with the parks and how the degree of satisfaction is related to demographic and behavioral variables.

   Hi_1: There was a relationship between user satisfaction with their preferred park and quality of park design, facilities, programs, and management.

2. To determine if the underlying causes of user dissatisfaction, if any, may have been due to a lack of coordination in the agencies:

   Hi_2: If there was public dissatisfaction with the design, facilities, programs, and management, then this may have been related to a lack of coordination between the planning and managing agencies.

The objectives of this research were approached through a two-part investigation. Objective 1 was studied through personal

36

interview questionnaires which probed user satisfaction with various aspects of the park. Objective 2 was explored through interviews with agency personnel designed to describe the coordination and communication between the agencies.

Finally, the results of the first two objectives are synthesized to form recommendations for recreation in Kuwait.

Design of the Interview Questionnaire

The personal interview used to collect data for this study was based on a standardized questionnaire to meet the first objective, to determine user satisfaction. In constructing the questionnaire, several factors were considered. These include the way the questions were asked, the reliability of the response, the respondent's bias and how to reduce that bias. Also, the researcher's biases in designing the questionnaire were examined. All of these factors determine the quality of the questionnaire and the information collected.

The purpose of the questionnaire in this research was:

1. To determine which park was most used and why, so that similar techniques can be applied in less used parks.
2. To determine the quality of park design and how to use that data for improving urban parks.
3. To collect data about park management and how people react to rules and regulations in order to develop better understanding between park managers and park users.
4. To collect data about the present facilities and how it can be used to meet the users' needs.
5. To determine the quality and quantity of summer recreational programs and how the data can be used to improve future programs.

A second questionnaire was designed to collect certain information from the involved agencies to meet the second objective relating to interagency coordination. This questionnaire was administered by the author and directed to: 1) the Department of Agriculture (Park Section); 2) Ministry of Municipality; and, 3) the Department of Recreation and Tourism. The purpose of this questionnaire was:

1. to collect information about the planning process for each agency;
2. to determine the degree of communication or coordination between the involved agencies;

3. to determine how decisions by one agency may have an affect on the decisions of other agencies in relation to recreation.

By combining the data gathered from the park users and the data gathered from the agencies, recommendations can be formulated that may assist the involved agencies, which could improve the decision making processes and result in higher user satisfaction.

Pretest

A pretest of the questionnaire and the interview procedures was conducted in Kuwait during the summer of 1979 to determine any inadequacies in the wording and the structure of the questions. The pretest was also used to find out whether the questions were asked in such a way that reduced the managers' bias. This was especially important since the questionnaires were translated from English to Arabic.

A random sample of 40 Department of Agriculture employees was chosen to test the questionnaire and the interviewing method. During the pretest, several questions were changed, and several questions were added.

A valuable part of the pretest interview was the discussion of the questions between the author and the respondents after they had answered the questions. The respondents were asked: 1) what the question meant to them; 2) what further ideas that they had that were not brought out by the questions; and 3) what his or her feelings were about the questions in general. The criticisms and suggestions were recorded and evaluated. Another pretest was conducted with only 10 persons randomly selected. At this point all the questions in the revised questionnaire were understandable (see Appendix I).

Sampling Techniques

Sampling is a method that can be used to collect information about a large population using only a small number of individuals from that population. The small sample must be viewed as an approximation of the population as a whole rather than a whole in itself (Moser and Kalton, 1971).

Sampling techniques can be classified into two categories,

38

nonprobability sampling and probability sampling. Nonprobability sampling is a technique where the probability of selecting a person or a unit is not known. This technique was not used in this research project.

Probability sampling is a technique where the probability of selecting a person or a unit is known. This technique includes the following:

1. Random Sampling: This is a method of selecting a sample from a whole population. This technique could have been used in selecting the sample in Kuwait City, because it would have given each person in the city an equal chance of being selected. To obtain a randomly selected sample, tables of random numbers can be used. However, this method was not used because of its high cost in collecting the information from the city population.

2. Stratified Sampling: Stratified sampling divides the population into units which are called subpopulations. A random sample can be taken from each unit. The procedure is described as stratified random sampling. Stratified sampling is not limited to stratification using only one variable. Rather, one can stratify a population using two or more variables simultaneously. Although this method is not strictly used in this research, the conceptualization of stratified sampling contributed to the research.

3. Systematic Sampling: A sample can be selected from a population based on every Kth person in the population. The K is determined by the sampling ratio which is a function of the population items to be sampled $\frac{n}{N}$. (Here n represents the sample number and N represents the population as a whole (Paul, 1967). It is an accurate method, especially when it is used in a homogeneous population. In this study, every fifth person was selected to be in the sample. The reason for using this method is because of its simplicity and accuracy.

4. Cluster Sampling: Cluster sampling is considered to be a simple random sampling in which the population is divided into one or more clusters or areas. A random sample can be selected from each cluster or area. The final sample then can be selected from the clusters (Bailey, 1978). The advantage of using cluster sampling is saving time and money. But the disadvantage is that it is not a single sample; it is more than one survey sample with a possibility of sampling error in each sample. This method is

not used in this research due to the high possibility of sampling error. But the concept of cluster sampling was useful to this research.

A combination of stratified and systematic random samples were used in this study in order to obtain a representative sample. The population was stratified by park users at three Kuwait City parks, government workers, and private businessmen. From each strata, every fifth individual as a park user or as a non-park user (potential user) was chosen. To determine the sample size which would provide representation in the results, a formula was selected through consultation with statisticians at Colorado State University. A sample size of 400 persons with a 5% probability of error was computed. The probability of error indicates that the sample may not be fully representative of the 101,454 persons living in Kuwait City, but it is an approximation of the city population. The formula used in determining the sample size was:

$$n = \frac{Npq}{(N-1)\,D+pq}$$

where:

N = population size (101,454)

p = population responding one way = .5
q = 1-p
D = $\frac{B^2}{4}$ where B is the desired bound on the error (.05%)

By applying the above formula and using the 1980 estimated population and the 5% probability of error, a sample size of 400 individuals can be used to represent Kuwait City population. To obtain accurate information, the sample should represent park users and also non-park users (potential users). The sample was divided into four units. From each unit a sample of 100 persons was randomly selected. Since there were three major parks in the city, each park was considered to be a unit. A sample of 100 individuals was randomly selected. This division made each park equally important. The fourth unit of the sample was collected from non-park users (potential users). This unit was divided equally into two parts. Fifty persons were randomly selected from government offices, and the other fifty were randomly selected from private businesses. By using this sampling technique, the probability of excluding any individual in the population was reduced.

The study was conducted during the month of June and part of July, 1979, as use of the parks is heavy during the summer months. The green landscape and the programs presented in the parks during the summer months attracted many people to the parks.

Administration of Questionnaire

Two employees from the Ministry of Planning were selected to distribute the questionnaire and to collect the data. The method used for collecting the data was the personal interview. Those people were trained in the interviewing techniques by the staff of the Ministry of Planning. Training was used to assure that in carrying out their work, the interviewers would act and react in a consistent manner to eliminate influenced answers.

The questionnaire was designed to take 15 minutes with each interview. But, due to people's interest in the survey, longer periods of time were usually spent. Therefore, it took more than four weeks to complete the survey.

The survey information was collected by the interviewers every day from 4 pm until 8 pm. The interviewers rotated between the three parks. During the interviewing period the author conducted several spot checks on the interviewers to assure proper administration in collecting the data.

After completing the parks sample, information was collected from the non-park users (potential users) during business hours. It took over five weeks for the data to be collected.

Interviewing the Agencies' Personnel

The second questionnaire was administered by the author through interviews with the people who were directly involved with Kuwait's parks during the summer of 1979. Questions were asked according to each agency's function in relation to Kuwait's parks.

One person was interviewed in each of the three different agencies concerned with parks: the Department of Agriculture (design); the Department of Recreation and Tourism (programs); and the Ministry of Municipality (management and facilities).

There were approximately nine questions asked of each responsible person in each agency. The questions were given to each agency but they were not answered according to each question but to all questions in general. The first interview was with Mr. R. Al-Bawab, Division Head of Parks and Maintenance, Department of Agriculture. The questions were:

1. What are the planning processes used in selecting and establishing a park?
2. What are the difficulties if any in selecting and establishing a park?
3. Who would be in charge of the design process?
4. Is the public involved in the design?
5. Who sets the rules and regulations?
6. Is there any communication between the Agriculture Department and the other involved agencies?
7. What are the major difficulties facing the parks in Kuwait?
8. Do you believe a joint committee from the three involved agencies working together would produce better parks and recreational programs?

The second interview was conducted with Mr. Saleh Shehab, Assistant Under Secretary of the Ministry of Information, and chairman of the High Committee for Tourism and Recreation. Eight questions were addressed to Mr. Shehab as follows:

1. When did the recreation program get started?
2. What was the reason for starting such programs?
3. Who is in charge of the programs?
4. Who chooses the programs?
5. Who supports the recreational programs financially?
6. Is there any communication with other agencies?
7. Do you believe the method of choosing programs is appropriate?
8. Do you believe a joint committee from the three involved agencies working together would provide better parks and recreational programs?

The third and last interview was conducted with one of the Ministry of Municipalities park personnel. There were eight questions directed to the park personnel. The questions were as follows:

1. Why should the Ministry of Municipality be in charge of the parks?
2. What prevents them from taking over the entire park system?

3. Who sets the rules and regulations?
4. Do the park managers have any training or experience in park management?
5. When people complained about the rules did you try to listen or modify some of the rules?
6. Do you believe those rules are appropriate?
7. Is there any communication between you and the other agencies?
8. Do you believe a joint committee from the other park agencies working together would provide better parks and recreational programs?

Statistical Analysis

Information collected from the sample was analyzed by the author using the CDC computer at Colorado State University and using the SPSS system. Chi-square and cross-tabulation techniques were used to treat the data.

Chi-square is a nonparametric technique used in this research to determine whether a statistically significant and systematic relationship exists between two or more variables (Sendecore and Cochran, 1976).

An alpha level of .05 was chosen to support or reject the hypothesis. Chi-square statistics were chosen primarily because data collected was ordinal and nominal in scale.

Part 4

The Study Area

The study area was located in Kuwait City. Situated at 48°00′ longitude and 29°22′ latitude, the northern part of the city faces into the southern part of Kuwait Bay. It is about 5.25 kilometers long and 2.63 kilometers wide. The 1975 census indicated that the city's population was approximately 78,116 persons; 66,339 of whom were non-Kuwaiti and 11,777 Kuwaiti.

The city consists of five small districts: Dasman, Sharg, Murgab, Salhya, and Qibla (Figure 5). Residential areas, as well as business and commercial areas are present. Because of this arrangement, Kuwait City is used to represent the population as a whole based on the mixed nationalities, businesses, and public parks.

In Kuwait City there are two major public parks, Municipality Park and the Greenbelt Park. Greenbelt Park is divided into two smaller parks, the main portion, Greenbelt Park, and its extension, Sheraton Park.

The Municipality Park

This park is located in the center section of the business and commercial district of Kuwait City. Comprising an area of 35,000 square meters, Municipality was formerly a public cemetery until it was designated a park in 1961 because of the city's expansion. The task of designing the public park in busy downtown Kuwait began in

1962 when most of the graves were removed. The area is totally flat with no natural features or any vegetation. A 2.13 meters high wall was established as a park fence to protect the park from vandalism and misuse. Two main gates are to be open during the day and closed at night (Figure 6).

Within the park, there is a small restroom but no drinking fountain. The vegetation includes more than 1,000 trees, over 1,100 bushes and a grassy area of more than 25,000 square meters. In the center of the park stands a beautiful water fountain and many benches are located throughout the park. Water is pumped into the park for irrigation purposes. Seven laborers are assigned to irrigate and cut the grass. The Sulaibya water is brackish containing 5,000 parts per million of salt. It is not considered suitable for drinking.

Paths through the park are paved and are about 8-10 feet wide. Outside of the fence the park is given a pleasant appearance by rows of coconut type palm trees (Washingtonia) which surrounded it. There are no facilities for children.

The park is bordered by three major roads. On the east lies Fahad Al-Salem Street, which consists of most of the commercial businesses. Also on the park's east side there is a taxi station which operates 24 hours a day. Saif Aldawla Street borders the south; the west side is marked by Ali Alsalim Street and is only two blocks from the sea. The north section is bordered by the old Kuwait commercial district and the money exchange market.

The location of the park is unique. It serves mostly all the old and new commercial sections of the city. There are few apartment buildings close to the park, therefore it is used mainly during the day by commercial district people. Because of this location it is considered the most crowded park during the day. But, due to unexplained rules, the park is open only from 4 pm to 11 pm daily.

The park is designed and managed by the Ministry of Municipality. The trees and shrubs are planted and maintained by the Department of Agriculture (Parks Section). The water fountain is designed and operated by the Ministry of Electricity and Water.

The Greenbelt

The Greenbelt is located in the southern section of Kuwait City. Originating as a noncommercial or residential buffer zone in 1958, it is used to separate Kuwait City from the rest of the country. The

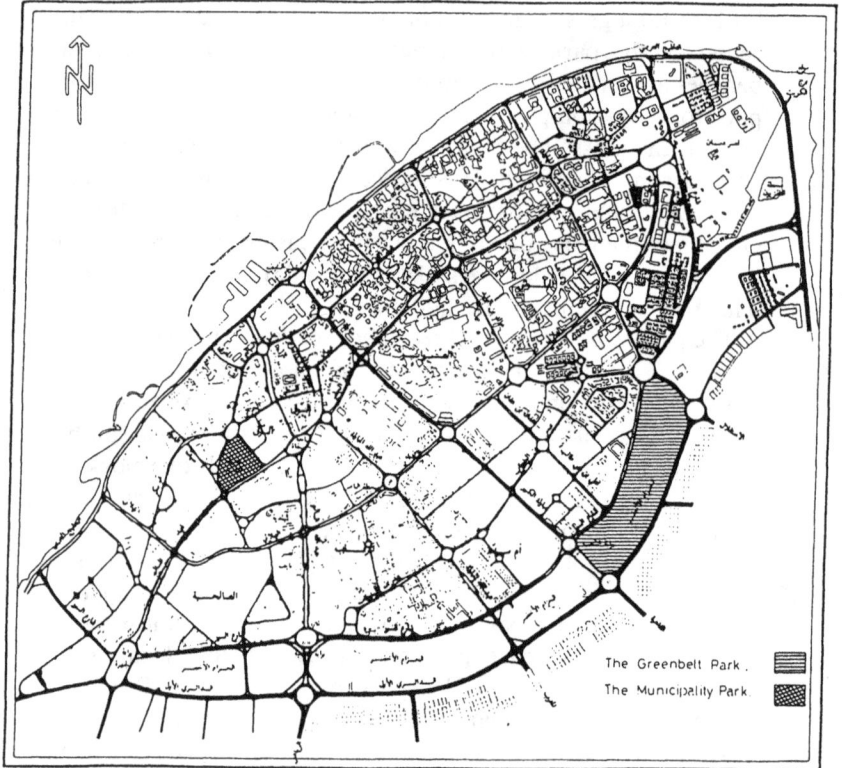

Figure 5: *The Greenbelt*

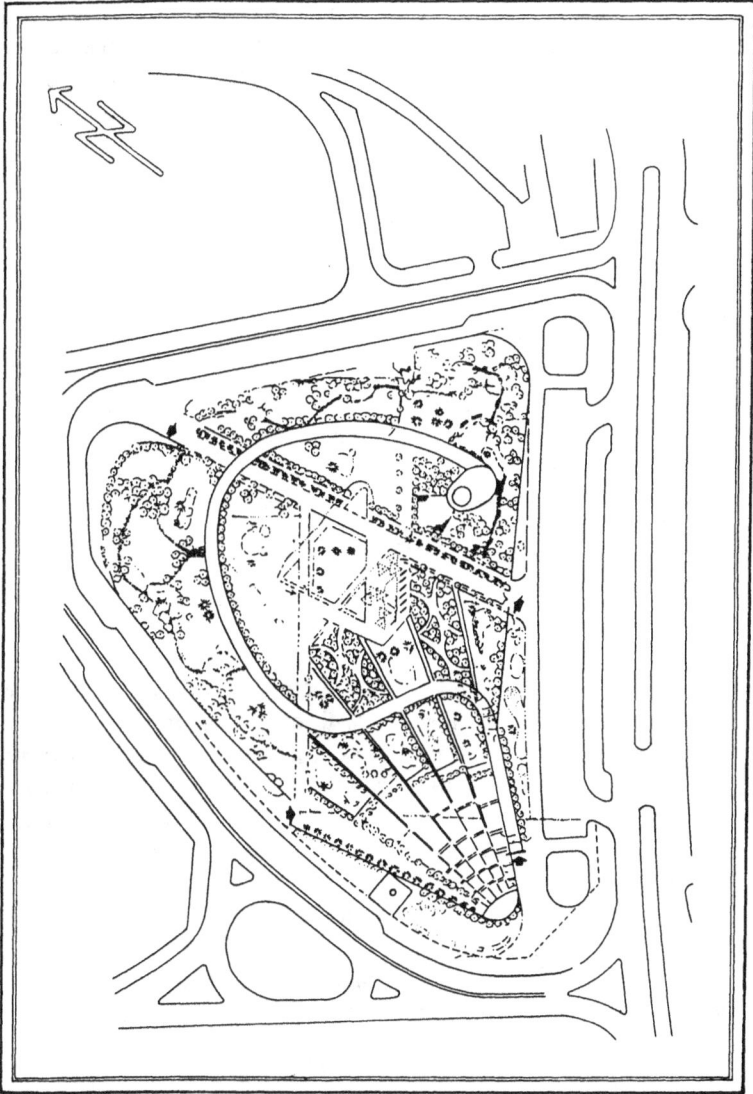

Figure 6: *The Municipality Park*

Greenbelt is a narrow strip of land that began in the southeastern section of Kuwait City where it meets the Gulf Coast Road. This 200-300 meter wide and 2.5-3.5 kilometer long park extends southwest until it again meets with the Gulf Coast Road at its western end. The Greenbelt is bordered on the south by five residential districts. Beneid Al-Qar, Dasman, Mansouriyah, Abdullah Al-Salem, and Shamiyah. Soor Street forms the park's northern boundary. The Greenbelt consists of four major parks which are the Greenbelt Park, the skating rink (completed during the fall of 1979), the Jahra Gate, and the Sheraton Park (see Figure 5).

The Greenbelt Park

The Greenbelt park was established in 1959 with an area of 200,000 square meters. The park is bordered on the east by Istiqlal Street and Beneid Al-Qar District, on the north by Soor Street and the commercial section of Kuwait City, on the south by First-Ring Road, Dasman District and Mansouriyah District and on the west by Cairo Street (see Figure 7).

The park is surrounded by a 2.13 meter high wrought iron fence containing four main gates. Two gates, located in the southern section of the park and facing First-Ring Road, are used as entrances. The other two gates usually remained closed. There are designated parking areas in front of the park. An information center is located in the southeast section of the park close to a main entrance. Also found here are cold water fountains, a restroom building with facilities for men and women, and a store that sells sandwiches and soft drinks. Other buildings found in the park included the offices of the Department of Agriculture in the southwestern section, a store (concessionaire) in the northwest section and a small building used for the guards by the fourth entrance gate in the northeast section.

The park is beautifully designed and landscaped. Half of its 200,000 square meter area is grassy space. There are more than 5,000 trees of different species and varieties as well as the 7,000 shrubs and bushes. The area is flat with no natural features. A large water fountain stands in the center of the park next to an amphitheatre used during the summer. The park contains a few secluded sitting areas surrounded by high shrubs, and a large network of paved walking areas. A 3 meter wide road extends the length of the park for sanitation trucks.

Six full time guards work in the park to protect it from vandalism
48

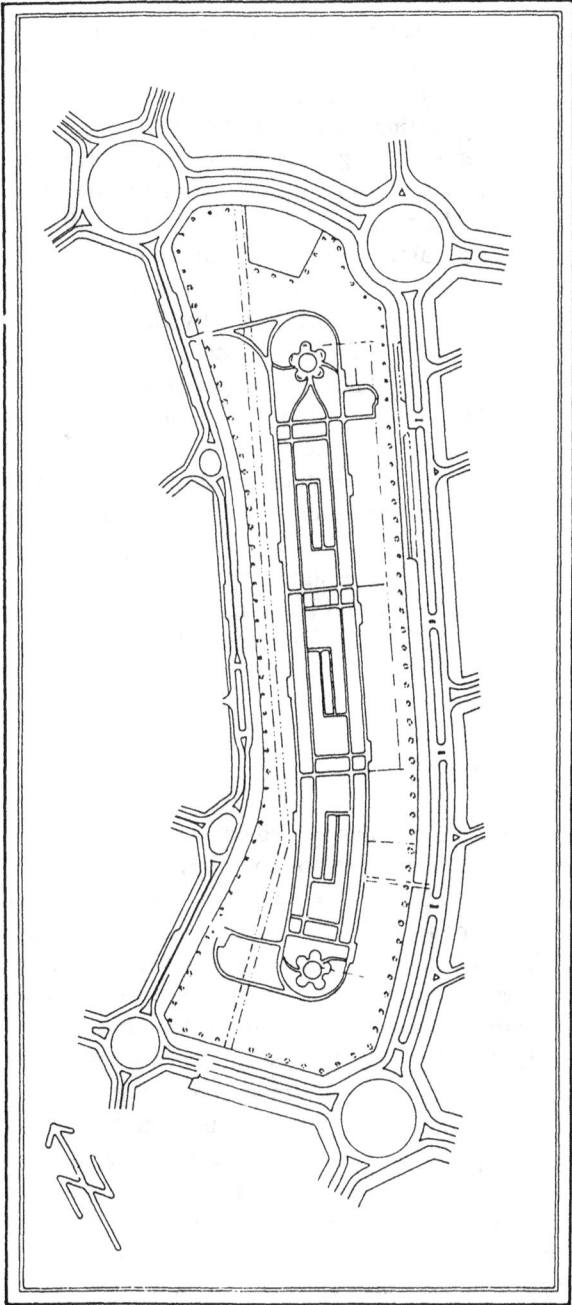

Figure 7: *The Greenbelt Park*

and misuse. These people are not trained or educated, but are employed because they can not find any other work, and are usually hired by the Ministry of Municipality. Twenty laborers work during the day irrigating, cutting the grass and planting flowers and bushes. A park supervisor is in charge of the general cleaning of the park and enforcing rules and regulations. This person and his staff are employed by the Ministry of Municipality. In 1979, he had little education and no training in park management.

In charge of Greenbelt and other parks within his district is the park superintendent. He is employed by the Ministry of Public Works. Department of Agriculture and supervises work in these parks. The park superintendent has special training in the field of horticulture and over 20 years of parks (public gardens) work, but no experience or training in the field of recreation.

The Greenbelt Park can be considered one of the most beautiful parks in Kuwait because of its design and landscape. During the summer, many recreational programs take place there. These programs were managed and paid for by the Ministry of Information, Department of Recreation and Tourism. The park users are a mixture of all segments of the population, especially Kuwait's citizens. The park is open for public use from 4 pm to 12 pm daily, free of charge.

The Sheraton Park

Sheraton Park is a triangular shaped park located at the western end section of the Greenbelt. It is bordered by Soor Street, the Sheraton Hotel and the largest Catholic church in Kuwait on the northeast; by Jehrah Gate on the southeast; by Jamal Abdul Nasser Street and the Shamiyah District on the south; and by Abu-beker Street on the west.

This park is surrounded by a 62 cm high wrought iron fence and occupies approximately 18,000 square meters. It has over 200 large trees and shrubs. The park contains a few benches, paved walking areas and a small restroom. There are no drinking fountains in the park and no programs during the summer (see Figure 5).

In 1979, the park was under heavy use by church members and hotel residents. On Sundays, it is considered the most crowded park in the country, however most of the users are non-Kuwaitis. In general, maintenance in the park is at a minimum level due to lack of interest by the Ministry of Municipality. There is only one laborer to irrigate the grass and prune the trees.

50

Part 5

Findings

Findings From Park Users and Potential Users

It has been suggested that a diversity among the involved agencies in the park planning effort in Kuwait exist. This diversity may have been created by a lack of cooperation or communication among the agencies. It has also been hypothesized that this uncoordinated management could be a factor in user dissatisfaction of the parks.

The findings in this part were obtained from analyzing the data collected by the interviewers and from interviewing the agencies' personnel.

Park Preferences

Part 1 of the questionnaire (Appendix 1) consisted of several introductory questions which asked about user preferences of urban parks. The people of Kuwait City were asked whether or not they had ever been in any of the city parks, which park was their preferred and which one was their least favourite. Over 80% of the sample had visited one of the three city parks. Less than 15% indicated that they were too busy or did not have time to visit any park. Table 1 shows detailed information about reasons for not visiting a park. According to the survey, the Greenbelt Park was the most preferred park in

Table 1. *Reasons given by potential park users for not going to any Kuwait City parks, 1979.*

Reasons	Frequency	Frequency %
I was busy	22	5.5
Crowded	6	1.5
Bad Management	4	1.0
No facilities	1	.2
Too far	7	1.7
Other	18	4.5
Not applicable	342	85.5

Table 2. *Resident ranking of most preferred Kuwait City park, 1979.*

Kuwait City Park	Absolute Frequency	Frequency %	Ranking
Greenbelt	276	80.0	1
Municipality	46	13.3	2
Sheraton	23	6.7	3

Table 3. *User reasons for liking or disliking most preferred Kuwait parks, 1979*

Elements	Element Most Liked (%)	Element Least Liked (%)
Design	64.3	6.4
Facilities	13.0	13.2
Programs	8.7	11.6
Management	2.3	44.3
No Opinion	11.6	24.1

Kuwait. Over 80% of those surveyed indicated that the Greenbelt was their most favorite. Municipality was the second favorite with over 10% of the use, and Sheraton was third with less than 8%.

Table 2 shows the sample distributions of preferences for Kuwait City parks. The respondents were then given five choices and asked to indicate what they liked or disliked about their favorite park. The five choices were park design, park programs, park management, park facilities, and no opinion.

The data indicated that over 60% of the respondents liked the design the best of their most preferred park, and little over 10% liked the facilities the best. In responding to what they disliked about their most preferred park, over 50% of the sample indicated the management and facilities were the reason.

Similar questions were asked about their least favorite park. Over 50% of the respondents indicated that the design was what they liked best about their least favorite park, and over 70% disliked the park because of the management and the facilities. Table 3 and 4 information about the favorite and least favorite parks.

Table 4. *User reasons for liking or disliking least preferred Kuwait parks, 1979*

Elements	Element Most Liked (%)	Element Least Liked (%)
Design	37.1	9.9
Facilities	3.2	62.3
Programs	.9	1.7
Management	.6	12.2
No Opinion	57.7	13.9

Visitation Pattern

Part 2 of the questionnaire (Appendix 1) was concerned with the length of time people spent in the park and the distance they traveled from their place of residence to the park. Data analysis indicated that there was no correlation between the two variables. Over 70% of the respondents spent two to five hours each visit, and over 80% lived from two to six kilometers from the park. Tables 5 and 6 show

Table 5. *Time spent by park users in most preferred Kuwait City parks, 1979*

Time Spent in the Park	Percent of Park Users
Less than 30 minutes	.3
30 minutes and more	2.3
One hour and more	11.9
Two hours and more	19.1
Three hours and more	18.8
Four hours and more	38.8
Five hours and more	8.7

Table 6. *Distance traveled by park users from place of residence to preferred Kuwait City parks, 1979.*

Distance Traveled From Place of Residence to the Park	Percent of Park Users
Less than half kilometer	1.4
Half a kilometer	4.9
One kilometer	12.8
Two kilometers	20.4
Four kilometers	18.6
Six kilometers	42.0

information about the time spent in the park and distance traveled.

Walking, sitting and talking, and watching their children were the major activities people enjoyed while in the park. Over 70% of the persons surveyed used the walking area, about 50% used the benches provided by the park and over 33% used the swings. However, less than 50% of the people used the restrooms.

In relating repeated visitation to the number of people found in the park at that time, about 90% of those who visited the park regularly said that the park was crowded or had a reasonable number of people (see Appendix 2).

Park Design

The third part of the questionnaire (Appendix 1) dealt with design related variables. The purpose of these questions was to determine whether or not the present design was adequate to meet user satisfaction. The information may be useful for future design.

In response to questions concerning the size of the park, over 65% of the people who were satisfied with the parks' design indicated the size of the parks were very large and about 12% said the parks were large enough, 3% said the parks were of medium size. Only 15% felt the parks were very small. Eighty percent of the Greenbelt Park users indicated the park was very large, 29% of the Municipality Park users said it was small, about 30% of the Sheraton Park users said the park was small and 52% said it was very small.

In relation to the availability of parking areas in the Greenbelt Park, over 78% indicated there are not enough parking areas during the weekdays and that the problem was worse on weekends. It is the only park with designated parking areas.

In relation to the park's fence over 70% of the park users indicated the height of the present fences was good because it kept children in the park. Only 10% said that the fence was very low, and this was in reference to the Sheraton Park. In response to questions concerning the walking areas, over 70% of the park users said the walking areas were good; less than 14% said that they were located poorly and this was in reference to the Municipality Park. Over 80% of the respondents indicated that there was enough sitting areas in the parks, however about 12% indicated there were not enough sitting areas in the park and this is in reference to the Sheraton Park (see Tables 7, 8, and 9).

Satisfaction with Design

Part 4 of the survey dealt with user satisfaction in relation to park design in general. The respondent was given five choices to indicate his/her level of satisfaction: highly satisfied, moderately satisfied, no opinion, moderately dissatisfied, and highly dissatisfied. The data indicated that over 80% of the respondents who returned to their favorite park were highly to moderately satisfied with the present park design in general. However, over 90% of the Greenbelt users were highly to moderately satisfied with the design, over 80% of the

Table 7. *Degree of user satisfaction with the elements of park design of the most preferred Kuwait City park, 1979.*

Degree of Satisfaction		Park Size				Parking Area				Park Fence					Walking Area			Sitting Area	
		1	2	3	4	1	2	3	4	1	2	3	4	5	1	2	3	1	2
Highly Satisfied	Ct	189	13	0	0	17	83	81	21	6	193	0	3	0	0	6	196	201	1
	R	93.6	6.4	0	0	8.4	41.1	40.1	10.4	3.0	95.5	0	1.5	0	0	3.0	97.0	99.5	.5
	T	68.5	4.7	0	0	6.2	30.1	29.3	7.6	2.3	73.6	0	1.1	0	0	2.2	71.0	73.1	.4
Moderately Satisfied	Ct	37	22	4	1	13	18	29	4	9	48	0	4	3	2	2	58	56	7
	R	57.8	34.4	6.3	1.6	20.3	28.1	45.3	6.3	15.8	84.2	0	6.3	4.7	3.1	3.1	90.6	88.9	11.1
	T	13.4	8.0	1.4	.4	4.7	6.5	10.5	1.4	3.4	18.1	0	1.4	1.1	.7	.7	21.0	20.4	2.5
No Opinion	Ct	0	4	1	0	1	0	4	0	0	4	1	0	0	2	0	2	1	4
	R	0	80.0	20.0	0	20.0	0	80.0	0	0	80.0	20.0	0	0	40.0	0	40.0	20.0	80.0
	T	0	1.4	.4	0	.4	0	1.4	0	0	1.5	.4	0	0	.7	0	.7	.4	1.5
Moderately Dissatisfied	Ct	1	0	0	2	0	3	0	0	0	2	1	0	0	0	2	1	0	3
	R	33.3	0	0	66.7	0	100.0	0	0	0	66.7	33.3	0	0	0	66.7	33.3	0	100.0
	T	.4	0	0	.7	0	1.1	0	0	0	.8	.4	0	0	0	.7	.4	0	1.1
Highly Dissatisfied	Ct	0	0	1	0	0	0	1	0	0	1	0	0	0	1	0	0	0	1
	R	0	0	100.0	0	0	0	100.0	0	0	100.0	0	0	0	100.0	0	0	0	100.0
	T	0	0	.4	0	0	0	.4	0	0	.4	0	0	0	.4	0	0	0	.4

Ct = count
R = row %
T = total %

Park Size
1 - Very large
2 - Large
3 - Medium
4 - Small
5 - Very small

Parking Area
1 - Enough
2 - Not enough
3 - Not enough on weekends
4 - No opinion

Park Fence
1 - High enough
2 - Block hot wind
3 - High enough, keeps children in
4 - Very low
5 - No opinion

Walking Area
1 - Very narrow
2 - Located poorly
3 - It is good

Sitting Area
1 - Enough
2 - Not enough

Table 8. *Degree of user satisfaction with the various elements of park design of second most preferred Kuwait City park, 1979.*

Degree of Satisfaction		Park Size					Parking Area				Park Fence					Walking Area			Sitting Area	
		1	2	3	4	5	1	2	3	4	1	2	3	4	5	1	2	3	1	2
Highly Satisfied	Ct	0	1	0	0	0	0	1	0	0	1	0	0	0	0	0	1	0	1	0
	R	0	100.1	0	0	0	0	100.0	0	0	100.0	0	0	0	0	0	100.0	0	100.0	0
	T	0	2.2	0	0	0	0	2.2	0	0	2.2	0	0	0	0	0	2.2	0	2.2	0
Moderately Satisfied	Ct	0	0	1	4	0	3	0	2	0	0	0	4	1	0	0	5	0	2	3
	R	0	0	20.0	80.0	0	60.0	0	40.0	0	0	0	80.0	20.0	0	0	100.0	0	40.0	60.0
	T	0	0	2.2	8.7	0	6.5	0	4.4	0	0	0	8.7	2.2	0	0	10.9	0	4.3	6.5
No Opinion	Ct	0	0	0	1	1	2	0	0	0	0	0	1	1	0	1	1	0	1	1
	R	0	0	0	50.0	50.0	100.0	0	0	0	0	0	50.0	50.0	0	50.0	50.0	0	50.0	50.0
	T	0	0	0	2.2	2.2	4.3	0	0	0	0	0	2.2	2.2	0	2.2	2.2	0	2.2	2.2
Moderately Dissatisfied	Ct	1	0	0	7	29	31	2	4	0	0	0	8	29	0	33	0	4	35	1
	R	2.7	0	0	18.9	78.4	83.8	5.4	10.8	0	0	0	21.6	78.4	0	89.2	0	10.8	94.6	2.7
	T	2.2	0	0	15.2	63.0	67.4	4.3	8.7	0	0	0	17.4	63.0	0	71.7	0	8.7	76.1	2.2
Dissatisfied	Ct	0	0	0	0	1	1	0	0	0	0	0	0	1	0	1	0	0	0	1
	R	0	0	0	0	100.0	100.0	0	0	0	0	0	0	100.0	0	100.0	0	0	0	100.0
	T	0	0	0	0	2.2	2.2	0	0	0	0	0	0	2.2	0	2.2	0	0	0	2.2

Ct = count
R = Row %
T = Total %

Park Size
1 - Very large
2 - Large
3 - Medium
4 - Small
5 - Very small

Parking Area
1 - Enough
2 - Not enough
3 - Not enough on weekends
4 - No opinion

Park Fence
1 - High enough
2 - Block hot wind
3 - High enough, keeps children in
4 - Very low
5 - No opinion

Walking Area
1 - Very narrow
2 - Located poorly
3 - It is good

Sitting Area
1 - Enough
2 - Not enough

Table 9. Degree of user satisfaction with the elements of park design of third most preferred Kuwait City park, 1979

Degree of Satisfaction		Park Size					Parking Area				Park Fence					Walking Area			Sitting Area	
		1	2	3	4	5	1	2	3	4	1	2	3	4	5	1	2	3	1	2
Highly Satisfied	Ct	0	0	0	1	0	0	0	1	0	0	0	0	0	1	0	0	1	0	1
	R	0	0	0	100.0	0	0	0	100.0	0	0	0	0	0	100.0	0	0	100.0	0	100.0
	T	0	0	0	4.3	0	0	0	4.3	0	0	0	0	0	4.3	0	0	4.3	0	4.3
Moderately Satisfied	Ct	0	0	0	6	12	2	6	8	2	0	2	0	4	12	2	0	16	6	12
	R	0	0	0	33.3	66.7	11.1	33.3	44.4	11.1	0	11.1	0	22.2	66.7	11.1	0	88.9	33.3	66.7
	T	0	0	0	26.1	52.2	8.7	26.1	34.8	8.7	0	8.7	0	17.4	52.2	8.7	0	69.6	26.1	52.2
No Opinion	Ct	0	0	1	0	1	0	0	1	1	0	0	1	0	0	0	1	0	0	2
	R	0	0	50.0	0	50.0	0	0	50.0	50.0	0	0	50.0	0	0	0	50.0	0	0	100.0
	T	0	0	4.3	0	4.3	0	0	4.3	4.3	0	0	4.3	0	0	0	4.3	0	0	8.7
Moderately Dissatisfied	Ct	0	1	0	0	1	0	1	1	0	0	0	1	1	0	1	0	1	0	0
	R	0	50.0	0	0	50.0	0	50.0	50.0	0	0	0	50.0	50.0	0	50.0	0	50.0	0	0
	T	0	4.3	0	0	4.3	0	4.3	4.3	0	0	0	4.3	4.3	0	4.3	0	4.3	0	0
Highly Dissatisfied	Ct	0	0	0	0	0	0	0	0	0	0	0	0	0	0	0	0	0	0	0
	R	0	0	0	0	0	0	0	0	0	0	0	0	0	0	0	0	0	0	0
	T	0	0	0	0	0	0	0	0	0	0	0	0	0	0	0	0	0	0	0

Ct = Count
R = Row %
T = Total %

Park Size
1 - Very large
2 - Large
3 - Medium
4 - Small
5 - Very Small

Parking Area
1 - Enough
2 - Not enough
3 - Not enough on weekends
4 - No opinion

Park Fence
1 - High enough
2 - Block hot wind
3 - High enough, keeps children in
4 - Very low
5 - No opinion

Walking Area
1 - Very Narrow
2 - Located poorly
3 - It is good

Sitting Area
1 - Enough
2 - Not enough

Table 10. *Summary of user satisfaction with park design, facilities, and management for Kuwait City parks, 1979.*

City Parks		Park Design					Park Facilities					Park Management				
		1	2	3	4	5	1	2	3	4	5	1	2	3	4	5
Greenbelt	Ct	202	64	5	3	1	13	181	13	69	0	14	121	8	131	2
	R	73.2	23.2	1.8	1.0	.4	4.7	65.6	4.7	25.0	0	5.1	43.8	2.8	47.5	.7
	C	99.0	73.6	55.6	7.1	50.0	100.0	91.9	81.3	61.6	0	87.5	95.3	72.7	2.4	20.0
	T	58.6	18.6	1.4	.9	.3	3.8	52.5	3.8	20.0	0	4.1	35.1	2.3	38.0	.6
Municipality	Ct	1	5	2	37	1	0	5	1	34	6	1	2	1	34	8
	R	2.2	10.9	4.3	80.4	2.2	0	10.9	2.2	73.9	13.0	2.2	4.3	2.2	73.9	17.4
	C	.5	5.7	22.2	88.1	50.0	0	2.5	6.3	30.4	85.7	6.3	1.6	9.1	18.8	80.0
	T	.3	1.4	.6	10.7	.3	0	1.4	.3	9.9	1.7	.3	.6	.3	9.9	2.3
Sheraton	Ct	1	18	2	2	0	0	11	2	9	1	1	4	2	16	0
	R	4.3	78.3	8.7	8.7	0	0	47.8	8.7	39.1	4.3	4.3	17.4	8.7	69.6	0
	C	.5	20.7	22.2	4.8	0	0	5.6	12.5	8.0	14.3	6.3	3.1	18.2	8.8	0
	T	.3	5.2	.6	.6	0	0	3.2	.6	2.6	.3	.3	1.2	.6	4.6	0

Ct = Count
R = Row %
C = Column %
T = Total

Degree of Satisfaction
1 = Highly Satisfied
2 = Moderately Satisfied
3 = No Opinion
4 = Moderately Dissatisfied
5 = Highly Dissatisfied

Municipality users were moderately to highly dissatisfied with the design, and over 80% of the Sheraton users were highly to moderately satisfied with the design (see Table 10).

To discover the relationship between satisfaction, design variables and demographic variables, a chi-square test was used. Tables 14 and 15 show information about the degree of satisfaction with park design, facilities, programs and management. The data indicated that over 80% of the Kuwaitis who were highly to moderately satisfied with the design had nine years of schooling or more. About 45% were male and over 33% female. Only 7% of the male Kuwaitis were moderately dissatisfied. In comparing Kuwaitis to non-Kuwaitis, over 60% of the non-Kuwaitis who were highly to moderately satisfied with the design also had nine years of schooling or more. Over 40% of the males and over 33% of the females were highly to moderately satisfied with park design (Appendix 3 shows detailed information).

Park Facilities

Part 3 contains a series of questions dealing with park facilities in general. Questions were asked concerning the presence of playing areas for adults and children. While over 60% of those who repeatedly visited their favorite parks felt that there was a need for designated playing areas for adults, less than 20% indicated that there was no need for these areas. However, about 80% of the park users felt that more facilities for children were needed.

Over 70% of the Greenbelt users, over 80% of the Municipality users and over 30% of the Sheraton users indicated a need for more facilities for children.

Because Moslem people pray five times a day, some of the parks in Kuwait have small designated praying areas. In Kuwait City parks there are no such areas; therefore, a question was asked concerning the designation of a small praying area. About 90% of the users indicated a need for these. Over 80% of the Greenbelt users, over 90% of the Municipality users and less than 50% of the Sheraton users indicated a need for designated praying areas.

As far as cooking in the parks, most of Kuwait's parks do not have grills and do not permit their use. However, a question was asked if people were interested in this type of facility. Over 60% of the returning users felt no need for grills in the park and only 13% showed any interest in having grills provided. Over 50% of the Greenbelt users, and 60% of the Municipality users, and over 70% of the Sheraton users indicated there was no need to use grills in the park.

Since there are no stores for refreshment in Sheraton or Municipality parks due to the surrounding business community, questions concerning store size in the park were only applicable to Greenbelt. Over 50% of the people sampled indicated that the store was very small to accommodate their needs. Twenty percent, on the other hand, indicated that the store was large enough.

The size of the restrooms located in the parks was not shown to relate to the park size or the number of users. But, due to the fact that in the Municipality Park, most of the restroom users were nonpark users, and since that might create a heavy use problem, it was appropraite to ask questions related to the size of the restrooms. Over 70% of those returning to their favorite park indicated a need for more restrooms, less than 25% indicated the restroom number was adequate.

However, over 60% of the Greenbelt users, over 90% of the Municipality users and over 60% of the Sheraton users indicated a need for more restrooms (see Tables 11, 12, and 13).

Satisfaction with Park Facilities

Part 6 of the questionnaire concerned user satisfaction with facilities (Appendix 1). The five point rating scale was used to measure satisfaction as described earlier. Fifty-six percent of those who returned to their favorite park were moderately satisfied with the facilities in general; less than 10% were moderately dissatisfied with the facilities (Appendix 4).

However, about 70% of the Greenbelt users were highly to moderately satisfied with the facilities and about 25% were moderately dissatisfied. Only 13% of the Municipality users were highly to moderately satisfied and about 85% were moderately to highly dissatisfied with the facilities. Less than 50% of the Sheraton users were moderately satisfied and about 43% were moderately to highly dissatisfied.

Chi-square was used to discover the relationship between satisfaction and facilities and demographic variables (see Tables 10, 14, and 15). The data indicated that 58% of the Kuwaitis who were highly to moderately satisfied with facilities had nine years of

Table 11. Degree of user satisfaction with various park facilities of most preferred Kuwait City park, 1979.

Degree of Satisfaction		Playing Area for Adults					Facilities for Children				Grills			Praying Areas			Concessions				Restrooms		
		1	2	3	4	5	1	2	3	4	1	2	3	1	2	3	1	2	3	4	1	2	3
Highly Satisfied	Ct	0	3	5	4	1	5	6	1	1	7	6	0	2	10	1	0	4	8	0	1	11	1
	R	0	23.1	38.5	30.8	7.7	38.5	46.2	7.7	7.7	53.8	46.2	0	15.4	76.9	7.7	0	30.8	61.5	0	7.7	84.6	7.7
	T	0	1.1	1.8	1.4	.4	1.8	2.2	.4	.4	2.5	2.2	0	.7	3.6	.4	0	1.4	2.9	0	.4	4.0	.4
Moderately Satisfied	Ct	0	3	132	37	9	10	157	4	10	31	121	29	1	176	4	1	111	60	9	0	66	115
	R	0	1.7	72.9	20.4	5	5.5	86.7	2.2	5.5	17.1	66.9	16.0	.6	97.2	2.2	.6	61.3	33.1	5.0	0	36.5	63.5
	T	0	1.1	47.8	13.4	3.3	3.6	56.9	1.4	3.6	11.2	43.8	10.5	.4	63.8	1.4	.4	40.2	21.7	3.3	0	23.9	41.7
No Opinion	Ct	0	0	9	0	4	0	6	0	6	0	9	4	0	10	3	0	8	0	5	0	5	8
	R	0	0	69.2	0	30.8	0	46.2	0	46.2	0	69.2	30.8	0	76.9	23.1	0	61.5	0	38.5	0	38.5	61.5
	T	0	0	3.3	0	1.4	0	2.2	0	2.2	0	3.3	1.4	0	3.6	1.1	0	2.9	0	1.8	0	1.8	2.9
Moderately Dissatisfied	Ct	0	1	55	7	6	0	64	1	4	9	47	13	2	59	7	0	60	1	8	1	1	66
	R	0	1.4	79.7	10.1	8.7	0	92.8	1.4	5.8	13.0	68.1	18.8	2.9	85.5	10.1	0	87.0	1.4	11.6	1.4	1.4	95.7
	T	0	.4	19.9	2.5	2.2	0	23.2	.4	1.4	3.3	17.0	4.7	.7	21.4	2.5	0	21.7	.4	2.9	.4	.4	23.9
Highly Dissatisfied	Ct	0	0	0	0	0	0	0	0	0	0	0	0	0	0	0	0	0	0	0	0	0	0
	R	0	0	0	0	0	0	0	0	0	0	0	0	0	0	0	0	0	0	0	0	0	0
	T	0	0	0	0	0	0	0	0	0	0	0	0	0	0	0	0	0	0	0	0	0	0

Ct = Count
R = Row %
T = Total %

Playing Area for Adults
1 - Adequate
2 - Not adequate
3 - There should be designated area
4 - There should not be designated area
5 - No opinion

Facilities for Children
1 - Adequate
2 - Need more
3 - No facilities, need some
4 - No opinion

Grills
1 - Like to have
2 - Don't like to have
3 - No opinion

Praying Area
1 - Don't need
2 - Like to have
3 - No opinion

Concessions
1 - Need one
2 - Small
3 - Adequate
4 - No opinion

Restrooms
1 - Should have one
2 - Adequate
3 - Need more

Table 12. *Degree of user satisfaction with the various park facilities of second most preferred Kuwait City park, 1979.*

Degree of Satisfaction		Playing Area for Adults					Facilities for Children				Praying Area			Grills			Presence of Store				Restrooms		
		1	2	3	4	5	1	2	3	4	1	2	3	1	2	3	1	2	3	4	1	2	3
Highly Satisfied	Ct	0	0	0	0	0	0	0	0	0	0	0	0	0	0	0	0	0	0	0	0	0	0
	R	0	0	0	0	0	0	0	0	0	0	0	0	0	0	0	0	0	0	0	0	0	0
	T	0	0	0	0	0	0	0	0	0	0	0	0	0	0	0	0	0	0	0	0	0	0
Moderately Satisfied	Ct	0	1	2	2	0	0	4	0	1	0	5	0	2	2	0	0	0	1	4	0	0	3
	R	0	20	40	40	0	0	80.0	0	20.0	0	100.0	0	40.0	40.0	0	0	0	20.0	80.0	0	0	60.0
	T	0	2.2	4.3	4.3	0	0	8.7	0	2.2	0	10.9	0	4.3	4.3	0	0	0	2.2	8.7	0	0	6.5
No Opinion	Ct	0	0	1	0	0	0	1	0	0	0	1	0	1	0	0	0	0	0	1	0	0	1
	R	0	0	100	0	0	0	100.0	0	0	0	100.0	0	100.0	0	0	0	0	0	100.0	0	0	100.0
	T	0	0	2.2	0	0	0	2.2	0	0	0	2.2	0	2.2	0	0	0	0	0	2.2	0	0	2.2
Moderately Dissatisfied	Ct	0	0	26	7	1	0	33	0	1	0	33	1	6	24	4	0	0	0	33	0	0	34
	R	0	0	76.6	20.6	2.9	0	97.1	0	2.9	0	97.1	2.9	17.6	70.6	11.8	0	0	0	97.1	0	0	100.0
	T	0	0	56.6	15.2	2.2	0	71.7	0	2.2	0	71.7	2.2	13.0	52.2	8.7	0	0	0	71.7	0	0	73.9
Highly Dissatisfied	Ct	0	0	5	1	0	0	6	0	0	0	6	0	2	3	1	0	0	0	5	0	0	6
	R	0	0	83.3	16.7	0	0	100.0	0	0	0	100.0	0	33.3	50.0	16.7	0	0	0	83.3	0	0	100.0
	T	0	0	10.9	2.2	0	0	13.0	0	0	0	13.0	0	4.3	6.5	2.2	0	0	0	10.9	0	0	13.0

Ct = Count
R = Row %
T = Total %

Playing Area for Adults
1 - Adequate
2 - Not adequate
3 - There should be designated area
4 - There should not be designated area
5 - No opinion

Facilities for Children
1 - Adequate
2 - Need more
3 - No facilities, need some
4 - No opinion

Praying Area
1 - Don't need
2 - Like to have
3 - No opinion

Grills
1 - Like to have
2 - Don't like to have
3 - No opinion

Concessions
1 - Need one
2 - Small
3 - Adequate
4 - No opinion

Restrooms
1 - Should have one
2 - Adequate
3 - Need more

63

Table 13. Degree of satisfaction with various park facilities of third most preferred Kuwait City park, 1979.

Degree of Satisfaction		Playing Area for Adults					Facilities for children				Praying Area			Grills			Presence of Store				Restrooms		
		1	2	3	4	5	1	2	3	4	1	2	3	1	2	3	1	2	3	4	1	2	3
Highly Satisfied	Ct	0	0	0	0	0	0	0	0	0	0	0	0	0	0	0	0	0	0	0	0	0	0
	R	0	0	0	0	0	0	0	0	0	0	0	0	0	0	0	0	0	0	0	0	0	0
	T	0	0	0	0	0	0	0	0	0	0	0	0	0	0	0	0	0	0	0	0	0	0
Moderately Satisfied	Ct	6	0	0	4	1	0	5	0	5	1	3	6	1	8	2	0	0	1	9	0	5	6
	R	54.5	0	0	36.4	9.1	0	45.5	0	45.5	9.1	27.3	54.5	9.1	72.7	18.2	0	0	9.1	81.8	0	45.5	54.5
	T	26.1	0	0	17.4	4.3	0	21.7	0	21.7	4.3	13.0	26.1	4.3	34.8	8.7	0	0	4.3	39.1	0	21.7	26.1
No Opinion	Ct	0	1	0	0	1	0	1	0	1	0	1	1	0	1	1	0	0	0	2	0	0	2
	R	0	50	0	0	50	0	50.0	0	50.0	0	50.0	50.0	0	50.0	50.0	0	0	0	100.0	0	0	100.0
	T	0	4.3	0	0	4.3	0	4.3	0	4.3	0	4.3	4.3	0	4.3	4.3	0	0	0	8.7	0	0	8.7
Moderately Dissatisfied	Ct	0	1	2	4	2	0	2	0	6	0	7	2	0	8	1	0	0	0	9	0	0	9
	R	0	11.1	22.2	44.4	22.2	0	22.2	0	66.7	0	77.8	22.2	0	88.9	11.1	0	0	0	100.0	0	0	100.0
	T	0	4.3	8.7	17.4	8.7	0	8.7	0	26.1	0	30.4	8.7	0	34.8	4.3	0	0	0	39.1	0	0	39.1
Highly Dissatisfied	Ct	0	1	0	0	0	0	1	0	0	0	0	1	0	1	0	0	0	0	1	0	0	1
	R	0	100	0	0	0	0	50.0	0	0	0	0	100.0	0	100.0	0	0	0	0	100.0	0	0	100.0
	T	0	4.3	0	0	0	0	4.3	0	0	0	0	4.3	0	4.3	0	0	0	0	4.3	0	0	4.3

Ct = Count
R = Row %
T = Total %

Playing Area for Adults
1 - Adequate
2 - Not adequate
3 - There should be designated area
4 - There should not be designated area
5 - No opinion

Facilities for Children
1 - Adequate
2 - Need more
3 - No facilities, need more
4 - No opinion

Praying Area
1 - Don't need
2 - Like to have
3 - No opinion

Preference for Grills
1 - Like to have
2 - Don't like to have
3 - No opinion

Concessions
1 - Need one
2 - Small
3 - Adequate
4 - No opinion

Restrooms
1 - Should have one
2 - Adequate
3 - Need more

Table 14. Degree of user satisfaction with design, facilities, programs, and managment of Kuwait City parks, by nationality and sex, 1979.

Degree of Satisfaction	Design				Facilities				Programs				Management			
	K*		NK*		K		NK		K		NK		K		NK	
	M*	F*	M	F	M	F	M	F	M	F	M	F	M	F	M	F
	%				%				%				%			
Hi-Satisfied	29	29	23	27	2	2	.7	.6	3.4	4.4	1.5	.8	2.4	2	2.3	0
Mod-Satisfied	15	8.2	17	8.1	26.5	28	24	25	24.4	16.6	19	18.2	22	1.8	17.4	16
No-Opinion	.9	0	.7	2	2	.8	4.3	3	9.3	9.3	17.4	18.2	2.4	.5	2.3	1.5
Mod-Dissatisfied	7	2.6	6	7.4	21	9	15.6	15.6	16.1	13.2	11.4	12.1	26.3	25	26	31.1
Hi-Dissatisfied	0	0	0	.7	.4	2	1.4	1.4	2	1.5	0	1.5	2	0	1.5	2.3

*K = Kuwaiti
*NK = Non-Kuwaiti
*M = Male
*F = Female

schooling or more. About 28% were males and 30% females. However, 32% of the Kuwaitis who were moderately to highly dissatisfied with facilities had nine years of schooling or more, and were 21% males and 11% females. In comparing Kuwaitis to non-Kuwaitis, about 50% were highly to moderately satisfied with facilities, and about 50% of them had nine years of schooling or more and only 5% had less than nine years of schooling. About 25% were males and 26% were females. About 34% were moderately to highly dissatisfied and had nine years of schooling or more and only 4% had less than nine years of school. About 17% were males and 17% were females.

Programs

Part 7 of the questionnaire dealt with the park programs (see Appendix 1). These programs were special activities organized and paid for by the Department of Recreation and Tourism, and offered to the public during the summer months in most Kuwaiti parks. These programs included concerts, plays, poetry reading, etc. The Greenbelt was considered to be a major park for providing such programs. Questions oriented toward the programs were concerned about whether or not people attended such programs, and for what reason. Questions were also asked about the quality of the programs in general. The data indicated that about 53% of those respondents attended a program. Of the people who attended a program, over 50% said they went especially to the park to see the programs, less than 30% indicated they didn't have a choice and about 10% said they just happened to be there. Over 50% of those who attended the programs said they need more and better programs, and about 33% said the present programs were good. Of those who did not attend any of the programs, over 50% said that they did not attend because of poor quality programs. The rest were either very busy or were not present in the country (see Tables 16, 17, and 18).

Satisfaction with Programs

Part 8 dealt with user satisfaction with programming (Appendix 1). In this section the respondents also rated their satisfaction on a five point scale. Less than 50% of those who attended programs were

Table 15. *Degree of satisfaction with design, facilities, programs, and management, of Kuwait City parks, by nationality and educational level, 1979.*

Degree of Satisfaction	Design K %		Design NK %		Facilities K %		Facilities NK %		Programs K %		Programs NK %		Management K %		Management NK %	
	HI	LO	HI	LO	HI	LO	HI	LO	HI	LO	HI	LO	HI	LO	HI	LO
Hi. Satisfied	48	5	54	7	1.7	2	1.3	0	4.4	3.4	2.4	0	3	2	2.3	0
Mod. Satisfied	22	4	21	3	50	6	47	5.3	37	4	32.3	4.5	33	6	32.3	.8
No Opinion	3	0	1	0	3	0	5.2	1.2	15	4.4	31.5	4	2.5	.5	2.3	1.6
Mod. Dissatisfied	12	2	7	3	26.3	4.3	28.4	4	26	3.4	20.3	3.8	45	6.3	47.4	10
Hi. Dissatisfied	1	0	0	.5	.8	.4	3	0	3.4	0	1.5	0	1.5	.5	4	0

K = Kuwaiti
NK = Non-Kuwaiti
HI = Hi educational level (nine years of schooling or more)
LO = Low educational level (less than nine years of schooling)

Table 16. *Resident reasons for not attending a program in Kuwait City parks by nationality, 1979.*

Resident Responses	Crowded			Bad Programs			Did Not Hear Of			Busy			Out of Kuwait			Do Not Care		
	Tot*	K*	NK*	Tot	K	NK	Tot	K	NK	Tot	K	NK	Tot	K	NK	Tot	K	NK
Number	86	52	34	21	13	7	7	5	2	25	10	15	9	5	4	15	8	7
Total %	50.9	55.9	48.6	12.4	14.0	10.0	4.1	5.4	2.9	14.8	10.8	21.4	5.3	5.4	5.7	8.9	8.6	10.0

* Tot = Total; K = Kuwaiti; NK = Non-Kuwaiti

highly to moderately satisfied with the programs and less than 30% were moderately dissatisfied with the programs. To determine the reliability of the data, correlations were checked between program variables, demographic variables and satisfaction. This was tested by chi-square to see if a significant relationship existed between the three (see Tables 14 and 15).

Of those people who went to the programs, 60% were Kuwaitis. Over 40% of them were moderately satisfied with the programs and less than 33% were moderately dissatisfied. The Kuwaiti sample was divided evenly; 50% being male and 50% being female. Over 33% of them had nine years of schooling or more and over 33% of those who indicated no opinion in the programs had the same schooling. On the other hand, about 50% of the non-Kuwaitis who saw a program were moderately satisfied. Over 25% of them said more and better programs were needed. About 25% who saw a program were moderately dissatisfied. Of the non-Kuwaitis, over 50% were female and about 40% were males. Chi-square indicated that there was no significant relationship between level of education and satisfaction with the programs (see Appendix 5).

Park Management

In part 9 of the questionnaire, the author investigated park management and related variables. The areas explored were that of the time the park was open, activity rules and regulations, and cleanliness of the facilities.

Most of Kuwait's parks have no specific regulations concerning opening and closing hours. Municipality Park and the Greenbelt are open from 4 pm to midnight seven days a week. When the respondents were asked about the present regulation of hours, over 70% indicated that they liked the present regulations. However, 20% of the respondents wanted to see the park open all day.

Some regulations might eliminate and restrict user activities while in the park. However, in most parks there are no written posted rules and often those that are written, are not clearly visible to the public. Over 40% of the park users said that they would like more flexible regulations and that some of the present regulations should be eliminated. On the other hand, a similar percentage indicated that they approved of the current regulations. However, 90% of the respondents indicated the need for written regulations.

Table 17. Reasons given by the respondents for attending a program in Kuwait's parks, by nationality.

	Went to See the Program			Free			Variety of Programs			No Choice			Happened To Be There		
	Tot*	K*	NK*	Tot*	K*	NK*	Tot*	K*	NK*	Tot*	K*	NK*	Tot*	K*	NK*
# of cases	89	61	28	3	0	2	10	7	2	10	7	2	23	17	6
Total %	49.2	54	43.8	1.7	0	3.1	5.5	6.2	3.1	29.3	23.9	40.6	12.7	15.0	9.4

* Tot = Total;   *K = Kuwaiti;   *NK = Non-Kuwaiti

Table 18. *Quality and quantity of programs as viewed by Kuwaitis and non-Kuwaitis.*

	Good Programs			Need More			Need More and Better		
	Tot*	K*	NK*	Tot*	K*	NK*	Tot*	K*	NK*
# of Cases	59	45	14	33	22	9	86	45	41
Total %	30.3	36.9	20.0	16.9	18	12.9	44.1	36.9	58.6

*Tot = Total;   *K = Kuwaiti;   *NK = Non-Kuwaiti

Table 19. Degree of user satisfaction with the elements of park management of most preferred Kuwait City park, 1979.

Degree of Satisfaction		Park Opening and Closing Hours				Regulations Eliminate Activities				Written Rules		Store Cleanliness				Restroom Cleanliness			
		1	2	3	4	1	2	3	4	1	2	1	2	3	4	1	2	3	4
Highly Satisfied	Ct	2	10	2	0	9	4	1	0	6	5	4	5	5	0	3	8	2	1
	R	14.3	71.4	14.3	0	64.3	28.6	7.1	0	42.9	35.7	28.6	35.7	35.7	0	21.4	57.1	14.3	7.1
	T	.7	3.6	.7	0	3.3	1.4	.4	0	2.2	1.8	1.4	1.8	1.8	0	1.1	2.9	.7	.4
Moderately Satisfied	Ct	1	102	17	1	75	34	9	3	15	105	2	91	19	9	1	44	56	20
	R	.8	84.3	14.0	.8	62.0	28.1	7.4	2.5	12.4	86.8	1.7	75.2	15.7	7.4	.8	36.4	46.3	16.5
	T	.4	37.0	6.2	.4	27.2	12.3	3.3	1.1	5.4	38.0	.7	33.0	6.9	3.3	.7	15.9	20.3	7.2
No Opinion	Ct	1	1	3	3	3	2	2	1	1	7	1	5	0	2	0	2	4	2
	R	12.5	12.5	37.5	37.5	37.5	25.0	25.0	12.5	12.5	87.5	12.5	62.5	0	25.0	0	25.0	50.0	25.0
	T	.4	.4	1.1	1.1	1.1	.7	.7	.4	.4	2.5	.4	1.8	0	.7	0	.7	1.4	.7
Moderately Dissatisfied	Ct	1	111	18	1	52	65	13	1	6	125	0	47	77	7	0	1	76	54
	R	.8	34.7	13.7	.8	39.7	49.6	9.9	.8	4.6	95.4	0	35.9	58.8	5.3	0	.8	58.0	41.2
	T	.4	40.2	6.5	.4	18.8	23.6	4.7	.4	2.2	45.3	0	17.0	27.9	2.5	0	.4	27.5	19.6
Highly Dissatisfied	Ct	0	0	1	1	0	1	0	1	0	2	0	0	0	2	0	0	0	2
	R	0	0	50.0	50.0	0	50.0	0	50.0	0	100.0	0	0	0	100.0	0	0	0	100.0
	T	0	0	.4	.4	0	.4	0	.4	0	.7	0	0	0	.7	0	0	0	.7

Ct = Count
R = Row %
T = Total %

Park Regulation
Opening and Closing Hours
1 - No regulation
2 - Like park regulation
3 - Park should be open all the time
4 - No opinion

Regulations Eliminate Activities
1 - Like present regulation
2 - Eliminate some

Written Rules
1 - Don't need any
2 - Need some

Store Cleanliness
1 - Very clean
2 - It is clean
3 - It is dirty
4 - Very dirty

Restroom Cleanliness
1 - Very clean
2 - It is clean
3 - It is dirty
4 - Very dirty

In response to the question concerning store cleanliness, over 50% said they found the store moderately dirty to very dirty. Less than 40% felt that the store was clean. The same question was asked about the restrooms. Over 70% of the sample said that the restrooms were moderately dirty to very dirty; less than 25% said they were clean (see Tables 19, 20, and 21).

Satisfaction with Management

Part 10 of the questionnaire was concerned about user satisfaction with the management. The five point rating scale was used to measure satisfaction as described earlier. Over 50% of the respondents said that they were moderately dissatisfied with the management in general; less than 40% said that they were moderately satisfied with the management. However, about half of the Greenbelt users were highly to moderately satisfied with the management, and over 90% moderately to highly dissatisfied. Only 7% of the Municipality users were highly to moderately satisfied with management, and over 90% were moderately to highly dissatisfied. About 22% of the Sheraton users were highly to moderately satisfied and about 70% were moderately to highly dissatisfied.

Chi-square was used to discover the relationship between satisfaction and management and demographic variables (see Tables 14 and 15).

The data indicated that 44% of the Kuwaitis who were highly and moderately satisfied with management had nine years of schooling or better and only 8% had less than nine years of schooling (25% were males and 4% females). About 54% were moderately to highly dissatisfied and had nine years of schooling or more and only 7% had less than nine years of schooling. About 28% were males and 25% females. In comparing Kuwaitis to non-Kuwaitis about 26% were highly to moderately satisfied with the management and had nine years of schooling or more, and less than 1% had less than nine years of schooling. About 20% were males and 16% were females. However, about 60% were moderately to highly dissatisfied with the management and had nine years of schooling or more. About 28% were males and 22% were females (Appendix 6).

Table 20. *Degree of satisfaction with the elements of park management of second most preferred Kuwait City park, 1979.*

Degree of Satisfaction		Park Opening and Closing Hours				Regulations Eliminate Activities				Written Rules		Store Cleanliness				Restroom Cleanliness			
		1	2	3	4	1	2	3	4	1	2	1	2	3	4	1	2	3	4
Highly Satisfied	Ct	0	1	0	0	1	0	0	0	1	0	0	0	0	1	0	1	0	0
	R	0	100.0	0	0	100.0	0	0	0	100.0	0	0	0	0	100.0	0	100.0	0	0
	T	0	2.2	0	0	2.2	0	0	0	2.2	0	0	0	0	2.2	0	2.2	0	0
Moderately Satisfied	Ct	0	2	0	0	0	1	1	0	0	2	0	1	0	1	0	0	1	0
	R	0	100.0	0	0	0	50.0	50.0	0	0	100.0	0	50.0	0	50.0	0	0	50.0	0
	T	0	4.3	0	0	0	2.2	2.2	0	0	4.3	0	2.2	0	2.2	0	0	2.2	0
No Opinion	Ct	0	0	1	0	1	0	0	0	0	1	0	0	0	1	0	0	1	0
	R	0	0	100.0	0	100.0	0	0	0	0	100.0	0	0	0	100.0	0	0	100.0	0
	T	0	0	2.2	0	2.2	0	0	0	0	2.2	0	0	0	2.2	0	0	2.2	0
Moderately Dissatisfied	Ct	1	10	22	1	15	15	2	2	2	31	0	0	0	34	0	0	7	26
	R	2.9	29.4	64.7	2.9	44.1	44.1	5.9	5.9	5.9	91.2	0	0	0	100.0	0	0	20.6	76.5
	T	2.2	21.7	47.8	2.2	32.6	32.6	4.3	4.3	4.3	67.4	0	0	0	73.9	0	0	15.2	56.5
Highly Dissatisfied	Ct	1	2	5	0	4	3	0	1	0	7	0	1	0	7	0	1	0	7
	R	12.5	25.0	62.5	0	50.0	37.5	0	12.5	0	87.5	0	12.5	0	87.5	0	12.5	0	87.5
	T	2.2	4.3	10.9	0	8.7	6.5	0	2.2	0	15.2	0	2.2	0	15.2	0	2.2	0	15.2

Ct = Count
R = Row %
T = Total %

Park Regulation Opening and Closing Hours
1 - No regulation
2 - Like park regulation
3 - Park should be open all the time
4 - No opinion

Regulations Eliminate Activities
1 - Like present regulations
2 - Eliminate some regulations
3 - Need flexible regulations
4 - No opinion

Written Rules
1 - Don't need any
2 - Need some

Store Cleanliness
1 - Very clean
2 - It is clean
3 - It is dirty
4 - Very dirty

Restroom Cleanliness
1 - Very clean
2 - It is clean
3 - It is dirty
4 - Very dirty

Table 21. *Degree of satisfaction with the elements of park management of third most preferred Kuwait City park, 1979.*

Degree of Satisfaction		Park Opening and Closing Hours				Regulations Eliminate Activities				Written Rules		Store Cleanliness				Restroom Cleanliness			
		1	2	3	4	1	2	3	4	1	2	1	2	3	4	1	2	3	4
Highly Satisfied	Ct	0	1	0	0	0	1	0	0	0	0	1	0	0	0	0	1	0	0
	R	0	100.0	0	0	0	100.0	0	0	0	0	100.0	0	0	0	0	100.0	0	0
	T	0	4.3	0	0	0	4.3	0	0	0	0	4.3	0	0	0	0	4.3	0	0
Moderately Satisfied	Ct	4	0	0	0	1	0	2	1	1	3	0	1	0	3	0	3	1	0
	R	100.0	0	0	0	25.0	0	50.0	25.0	25.0	75.0	0	25.0	0	75.0	0	75.0	25.0	0
	T	17.4	0	0	0	4.3	0	8.7	4.3	4.3	13.0	0	4.3	0	13.0	0	13.0	4.3	0
No Opinion	Ct	0	1	0	1	1	0	0	1	0	2	0	0	0	2	0	0	1	1
	R	0	50.0	0	50.0	50.0	0	0	50.0	0	100.0	0	0	0	100.0	0	0	50.0	50.0
	T	0	4.3	0	4.3	4.3	0	0	4.3	0	8.7	0	0	0	8.7	0	0	4.3	4.3
Moderately Dissatisfied	Ct	14	0	2	0	1	1	2	12	0	16	1	0	0	15	0	0	15	1
	R	87.5	0	12.5	0	6.3	6.3	12.5	75.0	0	100.0	6.3	0	0	93.8	0	0	93.0	6.3
	T	60.9	0	8.7	0	4.3	4.4	8.7	52.2	0	69.6	4.3	0	0	65.2	0	0	65.2	4.3
Highly Dissatisfied	Ct	0	0	0	0	0	0	0	0	0	0	0	0	0	0	0	0	0	0
	R	0	0	0	0	0	0	0	0	0	0	0	0	0	0	0	0	0	0
	T	0	0	0	0	0	0	0	0	0	0	0	0	0	0	0	0	0	0

Ct = Count
R = Row %
T = Total %

Park Regulations Opening and Closing Hours
1 - No regulation
2 - Like present regulation
3 - Park should be open all the time
4 - No opinion

Regulations Eliminate Activities
1 - Like present regulation
2 - Eliminate some regulation
3 - Need flexible regulation
4 - No opinion

Written Rules
1 - Don't need any
2 - Need some

Store Cleanliness
1 - Very clean
2 - It is clean
3 - It is dirty
4 - Very dirty

Restroom Cleanliness
1 - Very clean
2 - It is clean
3 - It is dirty
4 - Very dirty

Open-Ended Questions

Part 11 of the questionnaire consisted of open ended questions. Those questions were designed to obtain input from the users on the parks as a whole. Questions were asked about the kinds of activities which the users liked and that were not permitted by park regulation. Over 80% of the Kuwaitis wanted to play volleyball; 10% wanted to ride bicycles in the park. Ninety percent of the non-Kuwaitis wanted to play volleyball and less than 2% wanted to ride bicycles in the parks.

The second question asked about reasons for satisfaction, if any. Almost all of the sample indicated park design and park programs were major factors contributing to their satisfaction. When asked about what contributed to their dissatisfaction most of the negative reactions were directed towards the management and facilities. Over 27% of the Kuwaitis said that the restrooms were very dirty. Over 10% said that the park was dirty in general. The rest indicated a need for drinking water fountains. Of the non-Kuwaitis, about 20% said that their dissatisfaction was created by dirty restrooms and over 20% felt that the children's facilities needed repair. About 14% said the park in general was dirty and over 10% desired drinking water fountains.

The last open-ended question was designed to find out what facilities people wanted to see put into the parks. Twenty percent of the Kuwaitis said that they would like to see more and better facilities for the children. The desire for cold drinking water was indicated in almost every case. About 10% wanted more and better programs even though this was not an appropriate answer to the question. A very small percent indicated a need for law and order.

Comparing the above with the non-Kuwaiti population, about 25% of the females indicated a need for more facilities for the children. Over 7% wanted more and better programs. More than 20% desired tennis courts; over 20% indicated a need for drinking water fountains. About 10% said that they would like to see the fountain working (see Appendix 7).

Demographic Variables

Part 12 of the questionnaire (Appendix 1) collected the demographic variables of the sample population. About 54% of the respondents were male and 46% were female; 60% were Kuwaitis and 40% were non-Kuwaitis. The average age of the respondents was between 27 and 35 years. Over 50% were married and over 33% were single. Only 5% were widows and less than 2% were divorced. College students represented over 33% of the sample; over 33% of the sample had finished high school. Twenty percent had an intermediate level of education. Users' occupations included 20% students, 20% government employees, and over 15% housewives. Company employees, private businessmen, and merchants each made up less than 10% of the sample population (see Appendix 8).

The above information provides special information about the park users and their nationalities and whether the above data can represent the community as a whole. The demographic variables show whether the community is homogeneous or not so that we can determine the type of programs and what activities can be provided for the users.

Findings From Interviewing the Agencies' Personnel

Department of Agriculture

Mr. R. Al-Bawab indicated that there was no planning process in selecting and establishing any park in Kuwait. The Ministry of Municipality chooses the park location and the size of the park, because the Ministry of Municipality is in charge of all the public land in Kuwait. They also knew of all the existing residential areas in the country and the future ones. The process of communication for new parks is that a letter is sent to the Department of Agriculture informing them about the location of the new park. After receiving the location by the Department of Agriculture, a letter is sent to the Ministry of Electricity and Water asking them about the availability of water to the location. If the answer is positive then a committee will be set up for the design of the park. This committee usually consists of park personnel and architects from the Ministry of Public Works. After consulting with each other a draft for the park is presented. Modifications are made by the committee until they reach a final design. But, if the reply is negative from the Ministry of Electricity and Water, money will be allocated for the next year's budget to buy water for the park. When the money is approved then the design will begin. Also, money will be allocated for the park in general after the design is made.

Before the final approval of the park, if there are restrooms, water

77

fountains, and/or stores to be constructed, the Ministry of Municipality has to approve the location of those facilities. This usually creates a diversity of opinion among the people involved. Usually because of lack of interest and power, the Department of Agriculture usually agrees with the Ministry of Municipality's ideas. The Ministry of Municipality's design section criteria, however, differs from the Department of Agriculture's design staff criteria.

Mr. R. Al-Bawab indicated that most people were not pleased with the location of the above facilities because they were located near the entrance of the park. Many letters of complaint were received. According to him, the public is not involved in any way in the selection or designing of the park, because the public does not pay taxes or support the park by any means.

After the construction of the park, the park section of the Agriculture Department will be responsible for planting and irrigating the plants. The park usually is not opened to the public for the first two years due to the establishment of new grass and planting of new trees.

Since the park section budget does not allow for cleaning the park and facilities, the Ministry of Municipality is in charge according to the availability of money and manpower. It also set most of the rules and regulations.

Mr. R. Al-Bawab indicated that there are many difficulties which prevent the park system from improving. These are: 1) the low availability of water for irrigation prevents the establishment of new and bigger parks; 2) there are many agencies involved in the park system and each agency lacks the knowledge or expertise in park management or park planning; 3) there is no incentive for the park people to improve or increase their effort for making a better park; and 4) there is no strict law to punish the people who destroy the park and its facilities, even though there are guards in most of the parks. The guards' ignorance of the law prevents the citizens from being punished.

Finally, he indicated that a committee compiled from the involved agencies will not produce better parks. His statement was based on the fact that there is already a committee in existence where a lack of coordination among individual members still results in low quality parks.

Ministry of Information
Mr. S. Shehab indicated that the recreational program originated in

1973 when the Ministry of Information decided to provide recreational opportunities and programs for the citizens of Kuwait in Kuwait's parks, beaches and other recreational resources. Since most people of Kuwait leave the country during the summer months seeking other recreational opportunities, the Ministry of Information decided to provide some of those recreational opportunities free of charge to the public during the summer months in Kuwait's parks and theater. The Council of Ministers welcomed this new innovative recreational program idea. On July 6, 1973 approximately $200,000 was allocated for such programs.

A committee was appointed by the Minister of Information to select and control all the recreational programs in the country. Mr. S. Shehab was appointed as chairman of the committee. This committee usually consults with other government agencies about the variety of cultural programs to be presented to the public, consults with the radio and television agency about the quality of such programs, and the feasibility of broadcasting the programs on radio and television.

Mr. Shehab indicated there is a high level of communication between the Ministry of Information and most of the government agencies. During a park program the city police will be asked to keep law and order, the Boy Scouts will also be asked to help in assisting people during the programs, the Ministry of Municipality will clean the park before and after the programs and sometimes the Department of Agriculture, the park section personnel, will be asked to assist in providing plants in large containers to decorate the stage or be placed at the entrance of the park. The Agriculture Department involvement in the programming is very limited.

Mr. Shehab was asked whether the public should be involved in choosing the programs; the committee will try to provide programs for almost each segment of the population. Mr. Shehab explained that public support was a major factor for the success of the summer recreational programs. By receiving letters from the public, advising them or criticizing them for some of the programs, the committee will always try to provide quality programs for the whole population.

The success of the summer recreational programs made the government allocate more money for such programs. For example, the budget for the summer of 1979 was over $700,000. Mr. Shehab also indicated that they now are better and more experienced than the previous years.

The final question was asked if he welcomed the idea of a joint committee from other park agencies. He indicated that since they have the money and the personnel to do the job, it would be appropriate for them to select the programs and then ask for assistance from the other agencies. Mr. Shehab also indicated that at the end of each summer the committee will evaluate the programs and the operation, and set recommendations for the next year.

Ministry of Municipality

High administrator (who asked not to be identified) indicated that the reason they set park rules and regulations is because they don't have any other alternative. The Department of Agriculture did not want the responsibility of dealing with the public because they indicated that they were a technical information-oriented agency. Also, the Ministry of Information did not want the job because they operate only during two to three months of the year, that being the summer season. Therefore, since the Ministry of Municipality was responsible for cleaning the restrooms, cleaning the parks in general, maintenance and licensing of the stores, then it should be appropriate for them to set the rules and regulations. In addition, they have the money and the manpower to do the job.

They believe the entire park operation should be under their jurisdiction, but since they don't have the technical expertise in the field of horticulture, this technical job should be for the Department of Agriculture. On the question concerning the rules and regulations, they indicated that the rules were set by the Ministry of Municipality in consultation with the park section personnel of the Department of Agriculture. The rules were set to protect the park first and the people second. Since it is difficult to maintain good landscaping in the park, the rules should be restrictive in order to keep the park in good shape. The Agriculture Department insists on strict rules because maintenance costs are very high. Therefore, they have to see that those rules are followed by appointing managers who can enforce such rules. However, none of the park managers had any special training in park management nor do they know how to deal with people.

The reason for these managers having no training is because of the country's lack of professional instructors in park management and personnel who could train the managers. The Ministry of Municipality also believes those rules are appropriate because no one has complained even though no research has been done regarding the present rules.

The Ministry of Municipality also indicated there was a high level of communication with other involved agencies and especially with the Ministry of Information during the summer. But, they said little communication with the Department of Agriculture exists due to its attitude towards the parks. It indicated that the Agriculture Department's attitude toward the parks conflicted with the Municipality's attitude. The Department of Agriculture believes that the parks are only to beautify the city and not for public use. But the Ministry of Municipality believes that the parks should exist for public use and pleasure. Based on this conflicting attitude toward the parks created by little communication between the two agencies, the Ministry of Municipality believes a joint committee might produce better management and better parks. As stated previously, however, such a committee is already in existence and little, if any, coordination is taking place.

Part 6

Discussion of Results

Introduction

The purpose of this part is to analyze the results of the questionnaire data of previous parts to:
1. prove or disprove the hypothesis;
2. show the importance and implication of the findings to both users and managers, and;
3. show how the information can be used to improve Kuwait parks.

The following is a discussion of the design variables, facilities variables, programs quality and the management variables. This is related to the first hypothesis which stated:

Hi_1: There is a relationship between user satisfaction with their preferred park and their perception of the quality of park design, facilities, programs, and management.

In investigating this hypothesis, each component is discussed separately in order to find out how significant each component is in affecting overall user satisfaction with the park, and in order to make recommendations to the managing agency.

Satisfaction with Design

There are five elements in the park design that the research took into consideration. Each had varying affects on user satisfaction with the overall park design.

The design elements are size, parking area, fence, walking paths, and sitting areas.

Park Size

The survey showed that 66% of the park users indicated that the size of their most preferred park was very large. Twelve percent said the park was large and less than 15% indicated the park size was very small.

Their response can be related to the fact that all the neighborhood parks in Kuwait are less than 10,000 square meters in size (Department of Agriculture, 1979). This suggests that if any park is larger than their neighborhood park, it is thought to be very large. The Greenbelt Park (over 200,000 square meters), was indicated to be very large by 85% of users, the Municipality Park (25,000 square meters) as small by 69% of users, and the Sheraton (18,000 square meters) as small or very small by 85% of the users.

Their response to the large size can be substantiated by the high satisfaction level as the data indicated with the large size, the high number of users, and the high number of return visits to the Greenbelt Park.

The author agrees with the data that large size appears to be a positive feature because a large size park, such as the Greenbelt Park, provides adequate space for users to pursue their recreational activities, and reduces overcrowding under normal use. Besides these observations, the author's experience has shown that a large park also provides a more pleasant open space environment than small parks. The high number of trees and the large planted grass areas in the large park also could reduce the noise level in the park (Al-Mutawa, 1977). Cook and Haverbek (1972), conducted several experiments on noise reduction by using combinations of shelterbelts of tall trees and land forms. The indication was that noise could be reduced by half over a distance from 45 to 140 meters with a barrier consisting of trees. A decrease in the noise level also enhances users' recreational experiences. It appears that one of the major features in people's preference for their park is its large size.

It might follow then that a small park such as the Sheraton would have a negative effect on the user's park preference. Due to the relative closeness in size between the Sheraton and the neighborhood park, similar recreational opportunities are provided.

A relative increase in the number of users in a small size park could create overcrowding. The overcrowding then would result in an over use of the facilities and decrease the availability of the facilities for use. A small size park, such as the Sheraton Park, that has a limited number of trees, shrubs and grassy areas will not decrease the noise level in the park. A high noise level produces an unpleasant recreational environment, especially for those who seek quietness for relaxation.

The Municipality Park, on the other hand, was viewed by 12% of the sample as a large size park. The size of the park was three times larger than any neighborhood park. This relatively large park provided the users with more recreational opportunities than their neighborhood park. The park also has a considerable number of trees and grassy areas that reduced some of the noise level, and provided a pleasant recreational experience.

Response to size of park is also affected by whether the user is Kuwaiti or non-Kuwaiti. The Kuwaitis, in general, have more recreational opportunities to choose from than the non-Kuwaitis. As mentioned earlier, the Kuwaitis use the desert for recreational opportunities during the winter and spring seasons as an alternative to park use. During the summer, water-oriented recreational opportunities are also pursued. Therefore, if the park size is very small, some Kuwaitis will alter their recreational activities to the desert or to the sea.

Since most of the non-Kuwaitis are not familiar with desert-oriented recreational opportunities or have neither the time nor the money for water-oriented recreational activities, the parks are considered to be the only recreational environment for them to pursue their recreational activities. Seventy percent of the non-Kuwaitis indicated that their preferred park was very large. This was in response to the Greenbelt Park. The other 30% indicated their preferred park was small. This was in response to the Municipality and the Sheraton Parks.

About 75% of the Kuwaitis indicated that their preferred park was large; this was in response to the Greenbelt Park. About 10% said the Municipality and the Sheraton Parks were small.

The author believes that a small park can reduce the number of activities in the park. Also, a small increase in the number of users in a small park can create overcrowding that limits the number of activities that can be obtained in the park.

In conclusion, a small size park similar in size to the users' neighborhood park would have a negative effect on Kuwaitis, as well as non-Kuwaitis' experience and use of the parks. This is substantiated by the low number of user in the Municipality and the Sheraton parks. A small size park might have a positive effect on some users, but the data did not show that, while a large park would enhance Kuwait park users' recreational experience and use.

Parking Area

The availability of parking spaces to the park users affected their satisfaction level. The survey showed over 50% of the Greenbelt users indicating that the park was crowded, and over 40% indicated there were not enough parking areas during the week, or on weekends. The Greenbelt Park was the only park in Kuwait City that had a designated parking area. Lack of parking areas in the Municipality Park and the Sheraton Park had a positive as well as negative effect on park users. The positive effect was that the parks had fewer people and overcrowding was less of a problem.

For those who drive, lack of parking areas prevented them from using the Municipality and the Sheraton Parks. Most of the people who drive went to the Greenbelt where parking areas were available. The availability of parking spaces created a high demand for using the park and overcrowding at the Greenbelt.

Kuwaiti respondents and non-Kuwaitis had similar responses to the availability of parking areas. Limited availability of parking areas affected users negatively as unavailable parking spaces meant longer time for waiting for a vacancy. The long wait detracted from the recreational experience and satisfaction level with the park.

Park Fence

A high fence at the Greenbelt and the Municipality Parks enhanced park users' recreational experience and then added to their satisfaction level. Seventy-seven percent of the sample viewed the high fence surrounding the park as a means of keeping their children in the Greenbelt Park and the Municipality Park. The high fence made the park a safe environment for their children, and enhanced the users' recreational experience. About 11% said the fence is very

85

low, and this was in response to the Sheraton Park. The rest of the percent indicated no opinion or that the fence blocked the hot wind. Over 95% of the sample made repeated visits to their favorite park. However, 21.4% of the Sheraton Park users indicated the fence was very low. The author agrees with the data that park users viewed the low park fence as a hinderance to their experience, even though the park was located in an attractive area. Fifty-seven percent had no opinion concerning fences. The unsafe environment created discomfort among the Sheraton Park users because users have to keep constant watch on their children while they are in the park. The low fence then affected a significant number of park users' recreational experience negatively. There was no significant difference between Kuwaitis and non-Kuwaitis about the park fences.

Walking Area

The survey revealed that 77% of the parks' users indicated there were enough walking areas. Fifteen percent said walking areas were located poorly, and the rest had no opinion. The opportunity for using the city sidewalk for walking as a means of exercise or for recreation was very limited. As a result, most Kuwait parks provide walking areas designed to provide as much walking distance as possible without affecting the park shape or form (Department of Agriculture, 1979). The presence of the walking areas increased user recreational activities in the parks. The increase in the recreational activities by walking added to user satisfaction level with the park design in general. The survey indicated also that only 14% of the Municipality Park users were dissatisfied with the park design because of the poor location of the walking areas. However, 80% of the Sheraton Park users indicated there was enough walking area, 13% said walking areas were located poorly and about 7% had no opinion.

Thirteen percent of the non-Kuwaitis indicated the walking areas were located poorly. The author agrees with the data in response to the Municipality Park. Poorly located walking areas would affect a significant number of users' recreational experience. However, 62% of them indicated the walking areas were good. The rest had no opinion. Only 8% of the Kuwaitis indicated the walking areas were located poorly. Seventy-two percent said the walking areas were good and the rest had no opinion.

Summary

The analysis of the interview data indicated that 80% of the sample were satisfied with the parks' design in general, with only 12% dissatisfied. Of those Kuwaitis who were satisfied with the design, over 70% have more than nine years of education. There was no significant differences between Kuwaiti and non-Kuwaitis in terms of satisfaction with park design.

Over 90% of the Greenbelt users were satisfied with the design in general. This was likely due to the following elements of the design. People viewed a large size park as a positive element as it provides open space environments, more recreational opportunities, and quiet places. They also considered the high fence as a good element of the design as it makes the park a safe environment for the children. The walking areas were also an important element of the design as they provided park users with adequate areas for walking as a means of exercise and recreation.

They viewed the availability of parking areas of less importance than the other design elements. Even though it is difficult to obtain a parking space, user satisfaction level with the design was not affected. This was shown by their return visits to Greenbelt Park.

Over 80% of the Municipality Park users were dissatisfied with the design in general. This was probably a combination of the lack of parking areas that limit the recreational users, the poor location of walking areas, and park size. Even though the size of the park is not very large, the size then does not detract from their recreational experience as much as the previous elements. The users viewed the high fence as a positive element in the design as it provided a safe environment for the children.

Over 80% of the Sheraton Park users were satisfied with park design in general. For those that are not satisfied with design the most important element indicated was the low fence which made the park an unsafe environment for children, because of the high traffic in the area.

The data collected from the park users and potential park users, and the discussion support the first part of the hypothesis. As substantiated by the data, the author agrees that positive and negative elements of design would have a positive or negative effect on the park users. The degree of satisfaction should vary between the park users, according to their recreational needs. Further, the data shows that there was a positive as well as negative relationship

87

between users' satisfaction with preferred park, and perception of the quality of the park design. The Department of Agriculture, as the planning agency, should take into consideration each element of the park design and evaluate them according to the findings. Using the Greenbelt as a guideline for future park design, with some expansion to the parking facilities, a change in the design of the Municipality and the Sheraton Parks is not considered appropriate due to their location and their size. However, a complete study should be conducted if changes are required for the two parks.

Satisfaction with Park Facilities

There were six facilities that the study investigated. Each had varying effects on user satisfaction with the overall park facilities. The park facilities were: playing areas for adults, facilities for children, praying areas, grills, store, and restrooms.

Playing Areas for Adults

None of the urban parks in Kuwait had a designated adult area for playing (i.e., volleyball, tennis, etc.). The rules and regulations do not permit running as a means of exercise, or any sports-oriented activities in the park. The interviews with Mr. Al-Bawab, Department of Agriculture (1979), indicated that Kuwait parks were meant to beautify the cities and not for recreational activities. The department still holds the same attitude towards the parks. As a result, the study showed that over 70% of the sample indicated that their satisfaction level with the facilities was affected negatively by the absence of the adult playing areas. The author believes the absence of adult playing areas restricted users' recreational activities in the park.

Kuwaitis, as well as non-Kuwaitis, share similar responses concerning the absence of the adult playing areas. About 70% of each sample indicated that their satisfaction level with the facilities was affected negatively due to the absence of adult playing areas.

Although the Kuwaitis' recreational activities were affected by the absence of the adult playing areas, they have many alternatives to choose from. The author believes that Kuwaitis have no restrictions on joining any of the private recreational clubs, or any of the sports-oriented clubs. The availability of money also made water-oriented recreational activities easier to obtain. These alternatives provide more recreational opportunities, therefore, parks are lower in priority for Kuwaitis, for pursuing their recreational activity. But, for those Kuwaitis that cannot join any recreational clubs due to lack of money, the absence of the adult playing areas in the park reduced the number and the type of their overall recreational activities. Therefore, they are dissatisfied with the facilities in general.

The satisfaction level of the non-Kuwaitis with the facilities is affected negatively by the absence of the adult playing areas; since there are limited alternatives to choose from for recreational activities due to: 1) high eligibility requirements on joining private recreational clubs, or sports-oriented clubs; and 2) the limited availability of money to some people for recreational purposes. Dissatisfaction with the facilities will be the result when there is a lack of adult playing areas.

Facilities for Children

The study indicated that over 80% of the sample believe there were not enough facilities for the children in the parks. The Greenbelt Park was the only park in the city with facilities for children. The high ratio of children in the park and the limited number of facilities to be used created dissatisfaction with the facilities among the children.

The Kuwaiti sample is less affected by the limited number of children's facilities than the non-Kuwaiti sample. This can be explained, about 80% of the Kuwaiti population own a large home with recreational facilities for children (Kuwiat Census Report, 1975).

The non-Kuwaitis are more affected by the limited number of children's facilities. About 90% of the non-Kuwai'is live in apartments, and the remaining 10% rent homes from Kuwaiti residents. (A Kuwait law prohibits non-Kuwaitis from owning a home.)

Praying Areas

The absence of praying areas in the park affected most of the users' recreational experience. Over 90% of the sample indicated a need for a designated praying area. The absence of the proper facilities affected the duration of their stay in the park, and also affected their recreational experience. Users in most cases had to leave the park in order to pray at home or in a nearby mosque. Because of a short staying period in the park, less recreational activities would be obtained.

Restrooms

Over 70% of the park users indicated a need for more restroom facilities. The limited facilities created discomfort among park users. The location of the facilities created discomfort among parents, especially when children have to leave the park in order to use the facilities. The Municipality Park has only one restroom facility located outside the park fence. The Sheraton Park, with its heavy use on Sunday by church members, has no restroom facilities. The Greenbelt Park, with its limited number of restroom facilities, could not efficiently serve the park users due to the high number of users.

Kuwaitis, as well as non-Kuwaitis, viewed the restroom facilities the same. About 62% of each sample indicated a need for more restroom facilities. Twenty-three percent of each sample indicated a need for more facilities and the rest had no opinion.

Summary

The results from the interviews indicated that about 70% of the Greenbelt users were satisfied with the facilities in general. About 25% are dissatisfied with the facilities. The dissatisfaction is related to the limited number of children's facilities, the limited number of restroom facilities and the absence of the playing areas for adults.

About 85% of the Municipality users were dissatisfied with the facilities in general. Their dissatisfaction was related to the absence of facilities and the limited number of facilities.

About half the Sheraton Park users were satisfied with the facilities. Since there are no facilities in the park, the author believes that the facilities were not of great importance since the park was located near the Sheraton Hotel, and used by the hotel residents. The absence of the facilities were not important to them because of the availability of such facilities in the hotel. Some of the users were church members, who could use church facilities. But, for those who were not hotel residents or church members, 45% were dissatisfied with park facilities in general. The absence of all the facilities affected their satisfaction level negatively.

In general, the percentage of the Kuwaiti sample who were satisfied with the facilities was higher than the percent of the non-Kuwaitis from the same category. In looking at the negative relationship, the percent of dissatisfaction with the facilities among Kuwaitis and non-Kuwaitis was the same. Both populations view the absence or the limited number of facilities as negatively affecting their recreational experience in the park.

The data from the study and the discussion will support the second part of the hypothesis. The author again agrees with the data that the absence of adult playing areas, children's facilities, restroom facilities, and praying areas created a negative effect on park user satisfaction. However, the limited number of children's facilities and restroom facilities have a positive as well as negative effect on the park users. The degree of satisfaction will vary as indicated according to the user's religious background and cultural background.

The above information will assist the managing agency, the Ministry of Municipality, in better understanding the park users and their needs. By expanding the present children's facilities and restroom facilities, users' satisfaction will be increased. In providing restroom facilities, children's facilities, adult playing areas, and praying areas, the users' recreational experience in the park should be optimized. In optimizing the recreational experience, satisfaction with the facilities should be reached.

Satisfaction with Programs

In investigating user satisfaction with the parks' recreational programs, questions were directed to park users as well as to potential park users. Users' satisfaction was based on the 1978 recreational programs that were presented to the public free of charge in Kuwait urban parks, whether they were attending programs, reason for attending or not attending programs and quality of programs.

Programs Attendance and Quality

The results show that 52% of the sample attended some of the park recreational programs and 47% did not attend any recreational programs. Of those who attended the programs, 48% indicated the need for more and better programs. The author agrees with the data analysis that the public perceived the programs as of poor quality. The reason may have been due to the fact that the public is not involved in the selection process of the programs. This was substantiated by Mr. Shehab (1979) during his interview. He indicated that their budget was increased from less than $200,000 in 1974 to more than $700,000 for the summer of 1979, which was enough to present quality programs. He also indicated that the programs were selected by a committee from the Ministry of Information. The committee's intention was to provide quality recreational programs, but no study of the public's desires for recreational programs has been made.

Most of the programs presented in the parks are Kuwaiti-oriented (Ministry of Information, 1979), and are less interesting to the non-Kuwaitis. The findings show over 40% of them attended the programs because they do not have other alternatives. The author believes the reason of dissatisfaction was also related to poor quality programs first and because the programs were Kuwaiti-oriented secondly. However, there were non-Kuwaiti-oriented programs that were presented to the public in different locations other than the parks. The limited number of the seats that are available plays a limiting factor on the number of people that can attend such programs. As a result very few people will attend these programs. This also will contribute to users' dissatisfaction with the programs.

Kuwaitis also perceived the programs as of poor quality. The findings show about 40% indicated a need for more and better programs. Even though the programs are Kuwaiti-oriented, some of the programs are repeated year after year. This has been shown by the complaint messages the people send to the programs committee for improving the quality of the programs.

Another aspect of the programs' quality was the number of the programs that were presented. The recreational programs were not limited to the Greenbelt Park, but were presented in several Kuwait parks. Since Kuwait is a very small country, and gasoline prices are low, most people are able to attend most of the programs in any part of the country. But for those who are poor, or do not drive, traveling is difficult and expensive. This limited exposure or attendance to programs negatively affected their satisfaction level with the programs. This was reflected by 5% of the sample, as indicated by the need for more recreational programs than were presented during the summer in the Greenbelt Park.

For those who did not attend any recreational programs, over 50% indicated that the parks were crowded and prevented them from attending. Prevention from attending programs affected people's satisfaction negatively with the programs in general. The author believes crowding was the result of high number of people who are not living in Kuwait City but attending the programs. This is the result of the accessibility to the Greenbelt Park and the low price of gasoline.

Summary

About 45% of users sampled were satisfied with the programs in general; about 30% were dissatisfied. The dissatisfaction was related to the poor quality of programs, the limited number of the programs and the overcrowding of parks during a program. There was a higher percentage of Kuwaitis satisfied with the programs (48%) than non-Kuwaitis (40%). This is related to the type of programs that are presented and their relationship with Kuwaiti culture. The satisfaction or lack of dissatisfaction of the non-Kuwaiti to the programs can be explained by the fact that users have lived in Kuwait long enough so that they are accustomed to Kuwaiti culture and they have a better perception of the programs. There were also 32% Kuwaitis and 25% non-Kuwaitis who were dissatisfied. This can also be interpreted as the poor quality and the limited number of programs that were presented.

The above discussion agrees with the data analysis and supports the third part of the hypothesis. The managing and the planning agency for the recreational programs (the Ministry of Information), should use the above information to improve the quality of the programs. To do so, the public should be involved in the selection process. This can be done by either a direct public representation, surveys, or through suggestion boxes that should be located in every park where programs are presented. The suggestions are evaluation for each program. To improve the program's quality, a variety of programs should be introduced in the parks for both Kuwaitis and non-Kuwaitis. A survey should be conducted before the summer to obtain public ideas about the kind of programs that should be provided. Another survey should also be conducted at the end of the season to evaluate the programs. These should be done in order to improve future programs and the public satisfaction, and meet user needs.

Satisfaction with Park Management

There are five management elements that this study considered. Each element had varying effects on park user satisfaction with the overall park management. These elements were: 1) time of the day when the park opens and closes; 2) regulations that restrict recreational activities; 3) written rules; 4) store cleanliness; and 5) restroom cleanliness.

Time of the Day When the Park Opens and Closes

Most of the parks in Kuwait were open to the public from 4:00 pm until midnight. These regulations were set by the Department of Agriculture and the Ministry of Municipality Park Section. The reasons for such regulations were due to park maintenance activities. The maintenance activities were: irrigation, cleaning, and park maintenance.

Only 20% of the park users indicated that they would like to see the parks open all the time. The dissatisfaction of the 20% can be explained since the parks are only closed during the government working hours when most persons are employed. The author believes the regulations affected the housewives that are not working, the retired people and also the people who do not work during the day. Those people represent a very important segment of the population because they have the most leisure time to spend.

Kuwaitis as well as non-Kuwaitis viewed the regulations the same. Twenty percent of each indicated the parks should be open all day. Sixty percent of each liked the present regulation and the other 10% had no opinion.

Rules and Regulations

There are some park rules that prohibit users from playing ball, riding bicycles, running for exercise, or engaging in any other sports-oriented games. These rules are written on small signs at the entrance of the park. As a result of these rules, 40% of the park users said some of the rules should be eliminated. The author believes these rules are imposed on people's freedom to move in the park. In some cases, and especially during recreational programs, the authority for delegating the rules in the park is divided among several groups. Those include, the boy scouts, police, park personnel and the Ministry of Information personnel. This variety in personnel resulted in very strict enforcement. By eliminating some of the strict rules, users can pursue their recreational activities in the park, and satisfaction will be increased.

About 40% of the Kuwaitis and 40% of the non-Kuwaitis were negatively affected by park rules. As previously indicated Kuwaitis have many alternatives to choose from for obtaining their recreational needs other than the parks. However, the non-Kuwaitis were affected by the park rules due to the limited availability of money and other recreational opportunities. To them the parks are for relaxation, exercise and enjoyment. But, due to the restricted rules, many of their recreational activities were eliminated and their satisfaction level with the management reduced.

Store Cleanliness

One of the Ministry of Municipality's functions was to issue permits to the store in Greenbelt Park. The Ministry also inspected the store for its cleanliness and issued fines for the violators. Fifty-four percent of the sample indicated the store was dirty. The author believes the cause was heavy use from park users. Without continuous cleaning, the environment surrounding the store will be polluted with trash. Another reason for the dirty store was the leniency in rule enforcement by the inspector.

The users' recreational experience was affected by the dirty store environment; their satisfaction level with the management was affected negatively. Since about 44% of the sample indicated that the store is clean, the author believes those people used the store during the early hours when the park was opened, or they do not buy food or drink from the store. Therefore, their satisfaction level was not affected negatively.

Forty-six percent of the Kuwaitis indicated the store was clean, and 52% indicated the store was dirty. Of the non-Kuwaitis, 41% indicated the store was clean and 56% said the store was dirty. The missing percent had no opinion.

Restroom Cleanliness

The Ministry of Municipality, also was and is in charge of cleaning the park in general and the restroom facilities in particular. The park's restroom facilities were cleaned once a day during the morning. The limited number of restroom facilities and the heavy use by the park visitors caused dirty facilities before they are cleaned again. Eighty percent of the sample indicated that dirty restroom facilities were a source of dissatisfaction.

The restroom facilities are located outside the park fence at the Municipality Park. However, non-park users utilize them as well. Since the restroom facilities were cleaned only once a day, in the morning, the facilities became dirty before the park opened at 4 o'clock. About 90% of the Municipality Park users indicated dirty restroom facilities as a source of dissatisfaction.

Eighteen percent of the Kuwaitis indicated the restrooms were clean, and about 80% said the restrooms were dirty. However, non-Kuwaitis share similar response in that 15% indicated the restrooms were clean and 80% said the restrooms were dirty.

Summary

The data from the interviews show that 55% of the sample were dissatisfied with the management in general. Their dissatisfaction was caused by the restricted rules that reduce their recreational activities in the parks. Dirty environment surrounding the store and restroom facilities also affected their recreational experience in the parks

Kuwaitis and non-Kuwaitis viewed cleanliness the same. Their educational level had no effect on their perception of cleanliness.

The discussion supported by the data shows that the degree of user satisfaction with management quality was affected both negatively as well as positively. As a result, the findings support the fourth part of the hypothesis.

This information will assist the managing agency (the Ministry of Municipality) to understand the problem areas that caused user dissatisfaction. By improving problem situations, user recreational experience will be enhanced.

Inter-Agency Coordination and Communication

This discussion is related to the second hypothesis:

Hi$_2$: If there is public dissatisfaction with the design, facilities, programs and management, then this may be related to lack of coordination between the planning and managing agencies.

In investigating the second hypothesis, a content analysis of the interviews with the main personnel of the involved agencies was performed. Such an analysis revealed that lack of coordination was the result of conflict that affected the quality of the decision that the agencies had to carry out.

Conflict in Attitude

In discussing the agencies' attitudes toward the parks in general, the interviews with the agencies' personnel revealed that the Department of Agriculture believed that urban parks exist mainly to beautify the city and secondarily for public enjoyment and use (Al-Bawab, 1979). The author believes this attitude is strong in the Department of Agriculture, especially in the park section personnel and developed with the history of Kuwait. The desert climate in Kuwait permits little vegetation to grow naturally without irrigation. Therefore, the government policy was to plant trees, shrubs, and flowers mainly to beautify the country. Trees were also planted as windbreaks to protect the cities from the hot summer winds. To assist this effort many Kuwaiti individuals donated their private vegetated land to the government to enhance the country's visual landscape. Those private lands, with little alteration in the design and landscape by the Department of Agriculture, became public parks. The Department of Agriculture continued to see the parks as a means to beautify the country and not to provide recreational opportunities.

This attitude does not coincide with that of the Ministry of Municipality or the Ministry of Information. The two ministries believed that the parks are mainly for public use and pleasure, and secondarily to beautify the cities. The author believes this conflict in attitude created a lack of agreement between the agencies involved, especially in the area of establishing rules and regulations. The regulations were designed to protect the parks. However, some of the regulations created negative reactions by the park users. These

97

regulations eliminated some users' recreational activities, such as running, bicycle riding, sports-oriented games and others.

Coordination and Communication

Since most of the existing park rules were suggested by the Department of Agriculture Park Section, the Ministry of Municipality park personnel were, then, a means to achieve the Department of Agriculture's objectives, despite the conflict in attitudes. As a result, some of the rules were not enforced. The author believes the limited enforcement of the rules by the Ministry of Municipality park personnel created a conflict between the two agencies as to whether the rules should be enforced or not. This conflict, created by the incompatible attitudes toward parks, also hampered communication between the two agencies.

Another factor that the author believes contributed to lack of coordination between the agencies was the differences in the personnel of the agencies. The high level of education, specialization and status present in the hierarchy of the Department of Agriculture park personnel is in direct contrast to the lower education, lack of specialization or training in park management, and low status of the Ministry of Municipality park personnel. This results in poor communication, and the coordinating efforts are hampered. Although the Department of Agriculture park personnel enjoy higher status in the government hierarchy, they do not have any control over the Ministry of Municipality's park personnel and as a result less communication existed.

The Department of Agriculture also finds itself in similar conflict with the Ministry of Information. The Ministry of Information indicated that the public parks are for public use and for their recreational activities. This conflict creates a lack of coordination among the two agency's personnel despite the communication between them in the preparation of recreational programs.

Another contributing factor to the lack of coordination is maintenance costs. The author, as a park user and a government employee, knows that during the summer programs the urban parks are usually overcrowded resulting in heavy use of the facilities which continuously required maintenance. Overcrowding also damaged the park's landscape, which required additional time and funds for restoration. This continuous maintenance requires more money and manpower which the Department of Agriculture is responsible for providing. As a result, a deficit in the parks section budget is created, and when possible, money is borrowed from other projects just to cover the maintenance cost. However, money is not always available and the result was deteriorating facilities and poor quality parks.

The public usually praised the Ministry of Information for providing recreational programs, and criticized the Department of Agriculture for not maintaining the parks properly. The conflict between the two agencies not sharing the maintenance cost caused by the Ministry of Information limits future coordination between the two agencies' personnel.

An additional factor to the problem of poor maintenance was that the Department of Agriculture park personnel did not have any incentives to be creative or motivated toward better maintenance of the parks. To the park personnel the most obvious incentive that the Department of Agriculture could offer was an extra salary or wage during the busy summer season which was a normal condition of their employment. But, as a result of high maintenance cost, the incentive pay was eliminated for the park personnel (Al-Bawab, 1979).

In examining the relationship between the Ministry of Information and the Ministry of Municipality's park section, the author believes that both agencies share similar attitudes toward the parks. Both indicated that the parks were primarily for public use and their recreational activities, and secondly to beautify the cities. This common attitude brought them closer in providing public services. As previously stated, part of the Ministry of Municipality's duties are to prepare the parks before any recreational programs and to clean them afterwards. Yet, there are no extra operational costs to keep the parks clean. Also, the Ministry of Municipality park personnel receive extra pay every time a recreational program was presented. This incentive made park personnel eager to do a better job in providing their services for the park users.

The Ministry of Information, however, has similar benefits for their programs section personnel. The programs personnel receive extra incentive pay at the end of their recreational program seasons. This incentive made them work harder and better (Shehab, 1979).

The common attitude toward the parks between these two agencies and the incentive pay for their personnel results in good coordinated efforts by the personnel and created better communication between the two ministries.

Kuwait City Parks

The above discussion illustrates the problems caused by lack of coordination among the planning and managing agencies.

Part 7

Recommendations

There are three agencies involved in Kuwait's urban parks: the Department of Agriculture, Ministry of Municipality, and the Ministry of Information. Due to differences in their goals toward parks, and implementation of often conflicting goals, the users as well as the parks suffer. However, the author offers a set of recommendations that could assist the three agencies in implementing their decisions properly to benefit both users and parks.

The study indicates a strong need for better coordination among the related agencies in Kuwait. To help achieve better coordination the author suggests the formulation of a "Kuwait Park Coordinating Committee" consisting of representatives from each agency with a major responsibility in park administration. This committee should meet regularly to discuss current programs and problems. To reach a quality decision the committee should follow the decision making process model suggested Elbing (1970) and discussed on Page 15.

By recognizing the conflicts in goals that exist among the park agencies a conflict resolution should be adopted to reduce misunderstanding. Increasing the communication channels and improving coordination should result in better parks and satisfied users.

Recommendations for the Department of Agriculture from the Research Results

1. Due to the increasing public demand for recreational activities, the Department of Agriculture should adopt the policy that parks are for public recreational activities first, and to beautify the cities second.
2. In the process of designing a park, the Department of Agriculture should consult with the other two Ministries in order to have a better understanding about the location and the number of facilities needed, and also the type of programs to be presented.
3. Upgrade the Municipality and the Sheraton Parks by improving the maintenance programs to reduce litter and enhance vegetation appearance.

Author Recommendation

1. A management education program should be conducted to train the park personnel in the administration and management of parks.
2. Incentive pay should be part of agency policy for creative and productive employees. In obtaining creativity, Herzbuerg (1968) suggested that the management should enrich the employees' jobs. This can be done by upgrading of responsibility, scope and challenges in their work.
3. Mechanize the irrigation system in order to save time and money.

Recommendations for the Ministry of Municipality from the Research Results

1. Enforce all rules until the conflicting attitudes are resolved between the Department of Agriculture and the Ministry of Municipality.
2. Bigger signs are needed where the park regulations are posted in order to make it easier for the park user to recognize and read.
3. Insure user satisfaction with the facilities by seeing that the

restrooms are cleaned several times during the parks' opening hours.

4. The store manager must be strongly required to maintain a clean environment around the store in the Greenbelt Park.
5. The children's facilities should be expanded and maintained continuously in order to ensure children's enjoyment and safety.
6. Adult playing areas should be provided.
7. Small praying areas should be designated in each park.

Author Recommendation

1. Combine education programs with the Department of Agriculture to train park personnel in the administration and management of the parks.
2. Park guards should be trained to deal with the various publics.

Recommendations for the Ministry of Information from the Research Results.

1. The public should be involved during the process of program selection by interviews, surveys and representation on committees.
2. Research should be conducted dealing with the quality of the programs. Based on the research finding and evaluations, future selections of programs should be made.

Author Recommendation

1. The Ministry of Information should share part of the park maintenance cost after each summer program with the Department of Agriculture.

Overall Summary and Conclusion

The decision making process affecting Kuwait City parks has been fragmented between three agencies: the Department of Agriculture, the Ministry of Municipality, and the Ministry of Information. This fragmentation has been caused by conflicts in different goals, responsibilities and objectives. Each agency tried to implement its decision according to its main objectives. Because of different attitudes toward the parks in general, most decisions were unco-ordinated and made without any specific plan relating to the quality of the design, facilities, programs, or management. As a result, user satisfaction with the parks in general was affected both positively and negatively. This was evidenced by an 82% dissatisfaction with design in Municipality Park and a 96% satisfaction with the Greenbelt design. No efforts have been attempted to ease or resolve these conflicts.

Decision making is the process of choosing between alternatives and is the single most important function of the management. The author finds the three agencies neglected the important steps in the decision making for Kuwait parks. These steps move from the recognition of the problem, the clarification and analysis of the alternatives to the implementation of the decision (Simon, 1960; Elbing, 1970). Therefore, the entire decision making process must be completed before the implementation process.

Rationality is considered to be the key to good decision making especially in the public sector because it maximizes goal achievement with given environmental conditions (Gortner, 1978). However, if a decision is not reached due to certain environmental constraints, or due to conflict in choosing between alternatives, the conflict should be resolved first, and choosing between the alternatives second. This is not the case that exists in Kuwait parks during this study.

The results of this study show that users approved of park design in general more than they did park facilities, programs, or management. The author believes this was related to the specialization in the field of park design first, and to the wide exposure of park design personnel to European-urban parks design second.

Park users were also affected by park management and facilities in general. This was related to the duplication of facilities by the management from school and playground. Without any proper research and behavioral studies to what the users want, the result was user dissatisfaction. Park users were also affected by the poor quality programs that exist. This was due to the improper way of the program selection and program evaluation. About half of the users were dissatisfied with the programs.

In conclusion, the findings obtained from the users, and the discussion support the alternative hypothesis that there is a relationship between user satisfaction with their preferred park and the quality of park design, facilities, programs, and management.

Because of the conflict that exists between the managing and planning agencies due to the uncoordinated efforts by the agencies' personnel the quality of the park design, facilities, programs and management was affected.

Bibliography

Al-Bawab, Ramadan. Department of Agriculture, Kuwait. *Interview,* June, 1979.

Al-Mutawa, Subhi. *"Influence of shelterbelts on arid zone environment."* Unpublished Masters Thesis, Colorado State University, 1977, p. 93.

Arab Information Center. *The League of Arab States.* Kuwait: Kuwait Government Press, 1972, p. 12.

Bailey, Kenneth D. *Methods of Social Research.* New York: The Free Press, 1978, p. 478.

Bennis, Warren G. (ed.) *American Bureaucracy.* U.S.A.: Alpine Publishing Co., 1970, p. 187.

Berelson, Bernard, and Gary A. Steiner. *Human Behavior.* New York: Harcourt Brace and World, 1964, p. 377.

Blake and Mouton. *The Management Grid.* Houston, Texas: Gulf Publishing Company, 1969, p. 340.

Boulding, Kenneth. *Conflict and Defense.* New York: Harper and Row, 1963, p. 165.

Boris, Parl. *Basic Statistics.* Garden City, New York: Doubleday and Company, Inc., 1967, p. 218.

Brightbill, Charles K. *Man and Leisure.* Englewood California: Prentice Hall, Inc., 1962, p. 296.

Central Statistical Office, Ministry of Planning, Kuwait. *Annual Statistical Abstract.* England: Broadway Press Limited, 1978, p. 409.

Deatsch, Morton, "Conflicts: Productive and Destructive." *Journal of Social Issues*, XXV, January, 1969, p. 41.

DeGrazia, Sabastian. *Of Time, Work and Leisure.* Garden City, New York: Anchor Books, Doubleday and Co., Inc., 1964, p. 548.

Dewey, John. *How We Think*. Boston: D.C. Heath, 1933, p. 120.

Dregne, Harold E., (ed.) *Arid Lands in Transition*. Washington D.C.: American Association for the Advancement of Science, 1970, p. 524.

Elbing, Alvar D. *Behavior Decisions in Organization*. Glenview, Illinois: Scott, Foresman, 1970, p. 130.

Faludi, Andreas, (ed.) *A Reader in Planning Theory*. Oxford, England: Pergamon Press, 1973, p. 399.

Fenlason, Anne F. *Essentials in Interviewing*. New York: Harper and Brothers, 1952, p. 352.

Filley, Alan C. *Interpersonal Conflict*. Glenview, Illinois: Scott, Foresman and Company, 1975, p. 180.

Filley, Alan, and Robert J. House. *Managerial Process and Organizational Behavior*. Glenview, Illinois: Scott, Foresman and Company, 1969, p. 315.

Filley, Alan, Robert J. House, and Steven Kerr. *Managerial Process and Organizational Behavior*. Glenview, Illinois: Scott, Foresman and Company, 1976, p. 167.

Fishbein, Martin and Icek Ajzen. *Belief, Attitude, Intention and Behavior: An Introduction to Theory and Research*. Reading, Massachusetts: Addison Wesley Publishing Co., 1975, p. 578.

Fisher, Aubrey B. *Small Group Decision Making: Communication and the Group Process*. New York: McGraw Hill Book Co., 1974, p. 264.

Fuchs, Werner, Traugott E. Gattinger, and Herwig F. Holzer. *Explanatory Text to the Synoptic Geologic Map of Kuwait*. Vienna Austria: Gesellschaftsbuchdruckerei Bruder Hollinek, Wein, 1968, p. 87.

Gorden, Raymond L. *Interviewing: Strategy, Techniques, and Tactics*. Homewood, Illinois: The Dorsey Press, 1975, p. 587.

Gortner, Harold F. *Administration in the Public Sector*. New York: John Wiley and Sons, 1977, p. 343.

Gulick, Luther and L. Urwick (ed.) *Papers of the Science of Administration*. New York: Institute of Public Administration, 1954, p. 195.

Haas, Glen E. *User Preferences for Recreation Experience Opportunities and Physical Resource Attributes in Three Colorado Wilderness Areas*. Unpublished Doctoral Dissertation, Colorado State University, 1979, p. 141.

High Administrator, Ministry of Municipality, Kuwait. *Interview*, June, 1979.

Hornstein, Harvey A. and others. *Social Intervention: A Behavioral Science Approach*. New York: The Free Press, 1971, p. 597.

Jubenville, Alan. *Outdoor Recreation Management*. Philadelphia: W.B. Saunders Company, 1978, p. 290.

Kelly, Joe. *Organizational Behavior*. Homewood Illinois: Richard D. Irwin, Inc., and The Dorsey Press, 1974, p. 565.

Kraus, Curtis. *Creative Administration in Recreation and Parks*.

Kerlinger, Fred N. *Foundations of Behavioral Research*. New York: Holt, Rinehart and Winston, Inc., 1973, p. 741.

Kurohuma, Katsuzo and Yoshitaka Abe. *Fishes of Kuwait.* Tokyo: Dai Nippon Printing Co. Ltd., 1972, p. 123.

Litterer, Joseph, *Managing Conflict in Organizations.* Proceedings of the 8th Annual Midwest Management Conference, South Illinois University, Business Research Bureau, 1965, New York: MacMillan Company, 1969, p. 194.

Luthans, Fred. *Organizational Behavior.* New York: McGraw Hill Book Company, 1977, p. 588.

Luthans, Fred, and Kreitner. *Organizational Behavior Modification.* Glenview Illinois: Scott, Foresman and Company, 1975, p. 214.

Lynch, Kevin. *Site Planning.* Cambridge, Massachusetts: The M.I.T. Press, 1971, p. 384.

March, James G. and Herbert A. Simon. *Organizations.* New York: John Wiley and Sons, Inc., 1958, p. 262.

McLainghlin, William J. *The Indian Hills Experiment – A Case Study of Transactive Planning Theory.* Unpublished Doctoral Dissertation, Colorado State University, 1977, p. 306.

McFarland, Dalton. *Management.* New York: MacMillan, 1970, p. 83.

Meyer, Harold D., Charles K. Brightbill, and H. Douglas Sessoms. *Community Recreation: A Guide to Its Organization.* Englewood Cliff, N.J.: Prentice-Hall, Inc., 1969, p. 456.

Miller, William Dwain. *Planning Parks for Urban Growth: Fort Collins, A Case Study.* Unpublished Doctoral Dissertation, Colorado State University, 1973, p. 375.

Ministry of Information. *Programme of Tourism Recreation.* Kuwait, 1979, p. 70.

Morrow, William L. *Public Administration: Politics and Political System.* West Hanover, Mass: Halliday Lithograph, 1975, p. 272.

Moser, C. and G. Kalton. *Survey Methods in Social Investigation.* London: Heinemann Educational Books Ltd., 1971, p. 549.

Neumeyer, Martin H., and Esther S. *Leisure and Recreation.* New York: The Roland Press Co., 1958, p. 473.

Nie, Norman H. and others. *Statistical Package for the Social Science.* New York: McGraw-Hill Book Co., 1975, p. 675.

Parl, Boris. *Basic Statistics.* Garden City, New York: Doubleday and Co., Inc., 1967, p. 364.

Pondy, Louis. "Organizational Conflicts and Models." *Administrative Science Quarterly*, XII, September, 1967, p. 302.

Poulson, Roger I. *Methods of Interview Administration.* Unpublished Masters Thesis, Colorado State University, 1966, p. 99.

Richardson, Stephen A., Barbra Dobrenwend, and David Keleine. *Interviewing: Its Forms and Functions.* New York: Basic Books, Inc., 1965, p. 380.

Rodney, Lyn S. *Administration of Public Recreation.* Oregon: University of Oregon Press, 1964, p. 475.

Selltiz, Claire, Lawrence Wrightsman, and Stuart Cook. *Research Methods in*

Social Relation. New York: Holt, Rinehart and Winston, Inc., 1976, p. 624.

Schuman, David. *Bureaucracies, Organizations, and Administration.* New York: MacMillan Publishing Co., Inc., 1976, p. 235.

Shehab, Saleh. Ministry of Information, Kuwait *Interview*, June, 1979.

Siegel, Sidney. *Nonparametric Statistics for the Behavioral Sciences.* New York: McGraw Hill Book Company, Inc., 1956, p. 300.

Simon, Herbert A. *Administrative Behavior.* New York: The Free Press, 1976, p. 364.

Smith, Percy White. *The Planning, Construction and Maintenance of Playing Fields.* London: Oxford University Press, 1950, p. 224.

Snedecor, George W., and William G. Cochran. *Statistical Methods.* Ames, Iowa: Iowa State University Press, 1967, p. 593.

Tomas, John M., and Warren G. Bennis (eds.) *Management of Change and Conflict.* Baltimore: Penguin Books, 1972, p. 422.

Tompson, Victor A. *Modern Organization.* Alabama: The University of Alabama Press, 1977, p. 197.

University of Illinois, Department of Recreation and Park Administration. *The Leisure Attitudes, Interests and Behavior of Glencoe Park – Recreation District Residents.* Glencoe, Illinois: University of Illinois, 1967, p. 164.

University of Illinois, *The Leisure Behavior, Attitudes and Interest of the Citizens of LaSalle County District.* Ottawa, Illinois: University of Illinois, 1969, p. 290.

Van Haverbeke, David F., and Cook, David I. "Trees, Shrubs, and Landforms for Noise Control." *Journal of Soil and Water Conservation* 27(b) (November, 1972): 259-261.

Appendices

Appendix 1: Survey Questionnaire

1. Have you ever been in any Kuwait City parks?
     1. Yes ... Continue
     2. No ... Go to Question 11
2. What are the names of the parks you visited?
     1. Greenbelt Park
     2. The Sheraton Park
     3. The Municipality Park
3. What is your preferred park?
     1. Greenbelt Park
     2. The Sheraton Park
     3. The Municipality Park
4. Did you return?
     1. Yes
     2. No
5. What are the things that you like about that park?
     1. The design
     2. The programs
     3. The management
     4. The facilities
     5. Others
6. What are the things that you disliked about that park?
     1. The design
     2. The programs
     3. The management
     4. The facilities
     5. Others

7. What is your least preferred park?
    1. The Greenbelt Park
    2. The Sheraton Park
    3. The Municipality Park
8. Did you return?
    1. Yes
    2. No.
9. What are the things that you disliked about your least preferred park?
    1. The design
    2. The programs
    3. The management
    4. The facilities
    5. Others
10. What are the things that you liked about your least preferred park?
    1. The design
    2. The programs
    3. The management
    4. The facilities
    5. Others
    GO TO QUESTION 12
11. What are the reasons that you didn't go to any of the Kuwait City parks?

    1. Don't have time   5. No programs
    2. Too crowded   6. No facilities
    3. No parking area   7. Too far
    4. Bad management   8. Others
12. On an average visit how long did you stay in the park?

    1. Less than 30 min.   5. Three hours
    2. 30 min.   6. Four hours
    3. One hour   7. Five hours or more
    4. Two hours

SECTION 2

13. What activities did you engage in during your visit to that park?

    1. Walking   7. Riding a bicycle
    2. Picnicking   8. Reading
    3. Sightseeing   9. Resting
    4. Photography   10. Watching my children playing
    5. Playing cards   11. Others
    6. Sitting and talking
14. Are there any activities which you would like to engage in, which are not permitted at the park?
    1. Yes
    2. No

15. What are the activities in case of yes?
    1.
    2.
    3.
    4.
16. During your activities, what kind of facilities did you use?
    1. Chairs
    2. Grills
    3. Restrooms
    4. Swings
    5. Designated walking area
    6. Others
17. Are you satisfied with the facilities?
    1. yes . . . continue 18
    2. no . . . continue 19
    3. no opinion . . . continue 20
18. What is the reason for your satisfaction
    1.
    2.
    3.
19. What is the reason for your dissatisfaction?
    1.
    2.
    3.
20. What facilities would you like to have that are not available?
    1.
    2.
    3.
21. During your visit was the park
    1. Too crowded
    2. Acceptable number
    3. Not enough people
22. Does distance detract from your park experience and your use with regard to the number of times you return to the park?
    1. Yes
    2. No.
23. Is distance from your house to the park
    1. Less than ½ kilometer   4. 2 kilometers
    2. ½ kilometer   5. 4 kilometers
    3. 1 kilometer   6. 6 kilometers and more
24. Is that park (preferred park):
    1. Very Large
    2. Large
    3. Medium
    4. Small
    5. Very Small

25. In your visit to this park, was there a parking area?
    1. There is enough designated parking area.
    2. There is not enough designated parking area.
    3. Enough parking area during the week but not enough on holidays (Friday).
    4. No opinion (it does not make any difference).
26. Do fences around this park add or detract from your experience? In what way?
    1. The fence is high enough, blocking unpleasant scenery.
    2. The fence is high enough to block the hot wind.
    3. The fence is high enough to keep the children in.
    4. The fence is low. It does not block anything.
    5. No opinion (it does not make any difference).
    6. Others
27. Walking in this park may be one of your activities. The walking areas are:
    1. Very narrow
    2. Located poorly
    3. It is good, I like it
    4. Others
28. Sitting in this park may be one of your activities. The sitting areas are: Enough
    1. Yes
    2. No
29. The sitting areas are: Secluded
    1. Yes
    2. No
30. Please indicate how satisfied or dissatisfied you are with the design of the park.
    1. High satisfied
    2. Moderately satisfied
    3. No opinion
    4. Moderately dissatisfied
    5. Highly dissatisfied
31.
    affected
    1. The designated playing areas are adequate.
    2. The designated playing areas are small.
    3. There should be designated playing areas.
    4. There should be no designated playing areas.
    5. No opinion
    6. Others
32. Your preference for this park might also be affected by the presence or absence of facilities for children.
    1. There are enough facilities.

      2. Need more facilities

      3. No facilities for the children (need some)

      4. No opinion

33. Your preference for this park also might be affected by the presence or absence of the praying area.

      1. Don't need any

      2. Like to have a small designated area

      3. No opinion

34. Going to this park may require either to bring your own food or buying it. Would you prefer to have a few grills in the park for warming up or cooking your food?

      1. Yes, I would like to see a few grills put up in the park.

      2. No, I would not like it.

      3. No opinion

35. Your preference for this park may be affected by the presence or absence of a concession (store).

      1. There isn't any . . . need one.

      2. It is very small.

      3. It is large enough for the park visitors.

      4. No opinion

36. Your preference for this park may be affected by the presence or absence of restrooms.

      1. No restrooms (should have one)

      2. Enough restrooms

      3. Need more

37. Please indicate how satisfied or dissatisfied you are with the facilities in this park.

      1. Highly satisfied

      2. Moderately satisfied

      3. No opinion

      4. Moderately dissatisfied

      5. Highly dissatisfied

38. During the past summer there were many recreational programs presented to the public free of charge in some of Kuwait City parks. Have you attended any of these programs?

      1. Yes . . . Continue

      2. No . . . Go to Question 40

39. If yes, please check one.

      1. I went to the park because there was a program.

      2. I went to the park because it was free.

      3. I went because there was a variety of programs.

      4. I went because I didn't have a choice.

      5. I just happened to be in the park during a program.

      6. Others

40. If no, please check one.
    1. I didn't go because it was crowded.
    2. I didn't go because the programs were bad.
    3. I didn't go because I didn't hear about it.
    4. I didn't go because I was busy.
    5. I didn't go because I was not in Kuwait.
    6. I didn't go because I was not interested.
41. If you attended the programs, what is your opinion?
    1. The programs were good
    2. Need more programs
    3. Need more and better programs
42. Please indicate how satisfied or dissatisfied you are with the programs.
    1. Highly satisfied
    2. Moderately satisfied
    3. No opinion
    4. Moderately dissatisfied
    5. Highly dissatisfied
43. During your visit to this park, your preference for this park might have been affected by the regulations set by the management. This question deals with the time in which this park opens and closes during the day.
    1. There is no regulation.
    2. I like the park regulation.
    3. The park should be open all the time.
    4. No opinion
44. Your preference for this park might have been affected by the present regulations which restrict the types of activities you may participate in.
    1. I like the present regulations.
    2. Some of the regulations should be eliminated.
    3. Need more flexible regulations.
    4. No opinion
45. Your preference for this park might have been affected by the presence or absence of written rules and regulations.
    1. We don't need any.
    2. No written rules — we need some.
46. Your preference for this park might be affected by the cleanliness of the concession (store) area.
    1. I like it, it is very clean.
    2. I like it, it is clean.
    3. I don't like it, it is dirty.
    4. I don't like it, it is very dirty.
    5. No store
47. Also, your preference for this park might be affected by the cleanliness of the restrooms.
    1. I like it, it is very clean
    2. I like it, it is clean.

      3. I don't like it, it is dirty.

      4. I don't like it, it is very dirty.

48. Please indicate how satisfied or dissatisfied you are with the management.

      1. Highly satisfied

      2. Moderately satisfied

      3. No opinion

      4. Moderately dissatisfied

      5. Highly dissatisfied

49. Sex:

      1. Male

      2. Female

50. Which age bracket do you fall in?

      1. 12-15

      2. 16-20

      3. 21-26

      4. 27-35

      5. 36-45

      6. 46-55

      7. 56-65

51. Marital status

      1. Single

      2. Married

      3. Divorced

      4. Widowed

52. Nationality

      1. Kuwaiti

      2. Non-Kuwaiti

53. Educational level

      1. Illiterate

      2. Primary

      3. Intermediate

      4. Secondary

      5. College

54. Occupation:

      1. Student

      2. Housewife

      3. Laborer

      4. Merchant

      5. Government employee

      6. Company employee

      7. Private business

      8. Other

Appendix 2a. Number of residents who made a return visit to Kuwait City parks, 1979

Return	Absolute Frequency	Frequency %
Yes	399	98.3
No	6	1.7

Appendix 2b. Recreational activities participated in by users in Kuwait City parks, 1979

Activities	Absolute Frequency	Relative Frequency	Adjusted Frequency %
Walking	161	40.3	46.7
Picnicking	23	5.7	6.7
Sightseeing	28	7.0	8.1
Photography	19	4.7	5.5
Playing cards	17	4.3	4.9
Sitting, Talking	242	60.5	70.1
Bicycling	1	.2	.3
Reading	33	8.2	9.6
Resting	105	26.2	30.4
Watching Children	155	38.7	44.9
Others	91	22.7	26.4

Appendix 2c. User response to being crowded in Kuwait City parks last visit, 1979

Crowding Response	Absolute Frequency	Frequency %
Crowded	179	51.9
Reasonable Number	148	42.9
Not Crowded	17	4.9

Mean = 1.539 Std. Error = .033 Median = 1.464
Mode = 1.000 Std. Deviation = .619 Variance = .383

Appendix 3. Degree of user satisfaction with Kuwait City park design, 1979

Degree of Satisfaction	Absolute Frequency	Adjusted Frequency %
Highly Satisfied	204	59.1
Moderately Satisfied	87	25.2
No Opinion	9	2.6
Moderately Dissatisifed	42	12.2
Highly Dissatisfied	2	.6

Mean = 1.716 Std. Error = .060 Median = 1.346
Mode = 1.000 Std. Deviation = 1.105 Variance = 1.221

Appendix 4. Degree of user satisfaction with Kuwait City park facilities, 1979

Degree of Satisfaction	Absolute Frequency	Adjusted Frequency %
Highly Satisfied	13	3.8
Moderately Satisfied	197	57.1
No Opinion	16	4.6
Moderately Dissatisifed	112	32.6
Highly Dissatisfied	7	2.0

Mean = 2.719   Std. Error = .055   Median = 2.310
Mode = 2.000   Std. Deviation = 1.025   Variance = 1.052

Appendix 5. Degree of user satisfaction with Kuwait recreational programs, 1979.

Degree of Satisfaction	Absolute Frequency	Ajusted Frequency %
Highly Satisfied	19	5.5
Moderately Satisfied	136	39.4
No Opinion	87	25.2
Moderately Dissatisfied	94	27.2
Highly Dissatisfied	9	2.6

Mean = 2.820   Std. Error = .053   Median = 2.701
Mode = 2.000   Std. Deviation = .981   Variance = .962

119

Appendix 6. Degree of user satisfaction with Kuwait City park management, 1979

Degree of Satisfaction	Absolute Frequency	Adjusted Frequency
Highly Satisfied	16	4.6
Moderately Satisfied	127	36.8
No Opinion	11	3.2
Moderately Dissatisfied	181	52.5
Highly Dissatisfied	10	2.9

Mean = 3.122 Std. Error = .059 Median = 3.602
Mode = 4.000 Std. Deviation = 1.088 Variance = 1.183

Appendix 7a. Facilities that are not available in user's most preferred Kuwait City park, 1979

Facility/Support Service not Available		Kuwaiti		Non-Kuwaiti	
		Male	Female	Male	Female
More facilities	Ct*	7	19	1	9
for children	T(%)	9.5	26.5	2.6	24.4
Need cold water	Ct	13	6	13	6
	T	17.6	8.8	34.2	13.3
Need law and order	Ct	2	2	0	2
	T	2.7	3.0	0	4.4
Playing area for	Ct	11	8	8	0
adults (tennis cts.)	T	14.9	11.8	21.1	0

120

Facility/Support Service not Available		Kuwaiti		Non-Kuwaiti	
		Male	*Female*	*Male*	*Female*
Fountain should	Ct	3	4	1	4
be working	T	2.7	5.9	2.6	8.9
Park Maintenance	Ct	5	7	0	4
	T	6.8	10.3	0	8.9
More and better	Ct	11	6	0	3
programs	T	14.9	8.8	0	6.6

*Ct = count
T = total %

Appendix 7b. Reason for user dissatisfaction with facilities of the most preferred Kuwait City park, 1979

Reason		Kuwaiti %		Non-Kuwaiti %	
		Male	*Female*	*Male*	*Female*
Dirty Restrooms	Ct*	21	22	13	11
	T (%)	37.5	37.3	36.1	25.6
Fix Facilities	Ct	11	5	6	11
	T	19.6	8.5	16.7	25.6
Need more	Ct	3	5	2	4
Facilities	T	5.4	8.5	5.6	9.3
Dirty Park	Ct	4	4	4	7
	T	7.1	6.8	11.1	16.0
Need cold water	Ct	3	4	0	5
	T	5.4	6.8	0	11.5

*Ct = count
T = total %

121

Appendix 7c. Activities that are not permitted in most preferred Kuwait City park, 1979

Activities		*Kuwaiti %* Male	Female	*Non-Kuwaiti %* Male	Female
Ball	Ct	41	48	24	24
	T	76.7	81.4	88.9	85.7
Bicycling	Ct	5	4	2	1
	T	8.9	6.8	7.4	4.2
Grills	Ct	6	6	1	3
	T	10.7	10.2	3.7	10.7

Ct = count
T = total %

Appendix 8a. Distribution of Kuwait City park users by sex, 1979

Sex	*Absolute Frequency*	*Adjusted Frequency %*
Male	215	53.9
Female	180	45.1

Mean = 1.489   Std. Error = .031   Median = 1.428
Mode = 1.000   Std. Deviation = .613   Variance = .376

Appendix 8b. Distribution of Kuwait City park users by age, 1979

Age	Absolute Frequency	Adjusted Frequency %
12 - 15	31	7.8
16 - 20	54	13.6
21 - 26	62	15.7
27 - 35	104	26.3
36 - 45	80	20.2
46 - 55	45	11.4
56 - 65	20	5.1

Mean = 3.917   Std. Error = .080   Median = 3.990
Mode = 4.000   Std. Deviation = 1.587 Variance = 2.517

Appendix 8c. Distribution of Kuwait City park users by marital status, 1979

Marital Status	Absolute Frequency	Adjusted Frequency %
Single	144	36.4
Married	225	56.8
Divorced	7	1.8
Widow	19	4.8

Mean = 1.758   Std. Error = .037   Median = 1.740
Mode = 2.000   Std. Deviation = .734 Variance = .539

Appendix 8d. Distribution of Kuwait City park users by nationality, 1979

Nationality	Absolute Frequency	Adjusted Frequency %
Kuwaiti	240	61.5
Non-Kuwaiti	154	38.5

Mean = 1.404 Std. Error = .06 Median = 1.324
Mode = 1.000 Std. Deviation = .521 Variance = .272

Appendix 8e. Distribution of Kuwait City park users by educational level, 1979

Educational Level	Absolute Frequency	Adjusted Frequency %
Illiterate	33	8.3
Primary	23	5.8
Intermediate	81	20.5
Secondary	135	34.1
College	124	31.8

Mean = 3.742 Std. Error = .060 Median = 3.952
Mode = 4.000 Std. Deviation = 1.199 Variance = 1.437

Appendix 8f. Distribution of Kuwait City park users by occupation 1979

Occupation	Absolute Frequency	Adjusted Frequency %
Student	99	25.1
Housewife	63	16.0
Laborer	33	8.4
Merchant	26	6.6
Government Employee	80	20.3
Company Employee	37	9.4
Private Business	35	8.9
Others	21	5.3

Mean = 3.713   Std. Error = .114   Median = 3.577
Mode = 1.000   Std. Deviation = 2.269 Variance = 5.147

For Product Safety Concerns and Information please contact our EU
representative GPSR@taylorandfrancis.com
Taylor & Francis Verlag GmbH, Kaufingerstraße 24, 80331 München, Germany